HARTFORD 1944

HARTFORD 1944

A Story of Murder and Tragedy Under the Big Top

S. MICHAEL MCALLISTER

DEDICATION

For Paul, because a good friend is like a good book, *forever*.

ACKNOWLEDGMENTS

In remembrance of Eleanor Emily Cook.
She lay interned anonymously for
forty-seven years, known only as
Little Miss 1565.
The fire of July 6, 1944, took not only her life—but her name

So they took her form so light, Wrapped it in a cloth of white.
Laid it in a little grave, And the empty name they gave,
Was Little Miss Nobody.

There she lies a no-one still, Nameless on a lonely hill.
And the snowflakes and the rain, Come and go and fall again,
On Little Miss Nobody.

—Author unknown

Contents

Chapter 1

Janie Firefly

Janie was late for school. No matter how hard she tried, no matter how early she got up—it always amounted to the same. Janie was late for school. Take last night, for example, before her first day at her new school. Mother, a whirlwind as she laid out her school clothes, books, and pencils. Mother fussed about everything. Janie's shoes, socks, hair ribbons, but mostly Mother fussed about the India ink. Janie was eleven-years-old and enrolled in the fifth grade at Charter Oak Grammar School. This was the first year she was entrusted to use a fountain pen, and the specter of an insoluble black stain on her daughter's new school clothes loomed large in mother's mind.

"Mom! I know, okay, you told me hundreds of times. I'll be careful," Janie promised. Mother was somehow not reassured. Of all of Paula's four children, Janie was the one most prone to "accidents." Mother went into the kitchen to pack her lunch. One peanut butter sandwich on Wonder bread wrapped in crisp wax paper, a boiled egg, apple, and two oatmeal cookies, along with a thermos of milk, all packed neatly in Janie's Dale Evans lunch box.

"The cookies are for snack-time sweetheart, don't you dare eat them on the bus," Paula hollered from the kitchen.

"Gee mom, I know!" Janie crossed her fingers behind her back and cracked a sly grin. Holly J. did like oatmeal cookies, maybe just a nibble. Mother would never know. Janie sat on the back porch and dutifully polished her shoes. Well, she did manage to get one shoe (mostly) polished. Mother made such a fuss.

"Oh, Janie! What a mess!"

"Mom, it wasn't me. It was Seven!"

Mother remained unconvinced. "Not another word. Off to bed with you, young lady, you have a big day tomorrow."

"Aw, mom, it's almost time for Jack Benny!" Janie put on a sulk. "Go to bed."

This injustice by itself made Janie most powerfully provoked. Mother always had this dramatic way of making it seem like she wasn't even trying. *She was trying!* It was just that things didn't always turn out exactly the way she planned. Well, it wasn't as if it was all her fault. Her bestest-best friend in the whole world, Wednesday, was usually, mostly, sometimes to blame.

Wednesday and Janie were best friends since before kindergarten. The two girls were inseparable and did everything together. Wednesday was taller than Janie, with raven hair and bookish glasses. She was the kind of person to whom absolutely, positively every little thing in life was a monumental crisis. Wednesday's propensity for the dramatic, the dilemma, and the disaster often led Janie into big trouble. Wednesday always seemed to have some exciting distraction. If it wasn't an ancient Egyptian crypt to explore, or a mysterious voodoo curse to undo, it was some other, far worse, slithery miscreation to vanquish. Mostly, lately, all Wednesday could talk about was tales of saboteurs, assassins, and those shadowy Nazi spies.

Of course, getting up on time wasn't helped any when Janie spent the night before under the covers, reading the latest issue of *True Crime* by flashlight. It was all so terribly interesting. Janie whispered and giggled, as Wednesday turned the pages filled with astounding, astonishing tales of murder, U-boats, and Nazi saboteurs. Just think of it, the danger, the adventure, and all right here in New England.

What is a Nazi spy, anyway? Janie wondered. She decided she didn't quite know. Something bad, of that she was certain. What she did know was: the first time she'd ever heard of Nazi spies was when she listened to the grown-ups talking about 'em. Ever since Janie was enthralled with the whole notion of Nazi spies lurking unseen right here in Connecticut. She'd read the dire warnings about the dangers of Nazi spies in the *Hartford Courant.* From the looks of things, you'd think the entire countryside was veritably swarming with Nazis and their shadowy proxies.

Why just the other day, in front of Lang's drugstore, where Janie and Wednesday went to get nickel Nehis, in the window was a dramatic poster of a Liberty ship, the American flag flying gallantly. The ship was sinking, torpedoed. Janie spent more than a few vacant moments staring at the poster; she traced the outline of the shadowy, sinister submarine emblazoned with the Nazi swastika. The dire warning was clear: *Loose lips sink ships!*

"Come on," Wednesday whined. She jerked impatiently on Janie's sweater. "You gonna spend all day look'n at some dumb ol' poster?"

"I just might."

Wednesday put on a pout. Apparently, knowing that sinister submarines were lurking somewhere off the North Atlantic coast didn't quite fit with her grandiose scheme of a Nazi conspiracy. Janie sighed, and the two friends walked into Lang's drugstore and sat down at the soda fountain.

"Hello, Mr. Lang, two orange Nehis please," Janie said cheerfully in her bright sing-song voice.

Mr. Lang wiped a glass and peered over the tops of his spectacles at one very small little girl sitting alone at the soda counter. "Two orange Nehis?" Mr. Lang said slowly. The old pharmacist seemed confused.

Janie smiled sweetly. She twirled on the counter stool and from her handkerchief produced a whole dime to show she was earnest. Mr. Lang smiled faintly. From the ice chest, he brought out two frosty bottles of orange soda, popped the crown tops, and set them on the counter along with two straws and two napkins.

"Thank you, Mr. Lang." The two girls sat at the drugstore counter chatting; they sipped their orange sodas, all while Mr. Lang watched in amazement.

For the first ten of her eleven years, Janie lived in Calumet Heights, a suburb of Chicago. Janie missed living in Chicago, on account that's where her grandmother lived. Grams lived in the downstairs apartment, and Janie spent many happy afternoons sprawled on the friendly hardwood floor of her grandmother's cozy kitchen, poring over the well-worn pages of *The Book of Knowledge.*

On special days, Grams sometimes took Janie with her into the City. Those were the days Janie liked best. She got to ride in a taxi, and the exciting train ride downtown. Janie liked the way the colored doorman, Mr. Bixby, greeted them with his broad smile and perfectly white teeth.

"G' morn'n, Mrs. McConaughey." Mr. Bixby tipped his hat. He looked so very important, dressed in his dark green overcoat, resplendent with shiny brass buttons.

"G' morn'n, lil' Miss Janie."

"Good morning, Mr. Bixby. Guess what? Grams is taking me to see my *pee-atrician!*" Janie didn't notice the grown-ups snicker. The marvelous revolving door captivated her attention. She was so enthralled she went around twice.

"Janie, must you fool around so?" Grams was in a hurry.

Janie rejoiced in the hollow echo of the cavernous foyer as her shoes clicked on the polished marble. The elevator ride up, up thirty-five floors to Dr. Waldo's office fascinated her.

"Can I push the button, mister?" Janie watched as the operator worked the accordion gate and announced all the floors. That simply, positively must be the most glamorous job in the whole world. Janie decided when she grew up, she wanted to be an elevator operator.

Janie ran to the window. "Look Grams, you can see for miles!" It was all so very exciting that it almost made up for the inevitable sting of the vaccination.

For as long as Janie could remember, "Uncle Ted" (that was what the family called him), was her pediatrician. *"Wasting time, diddling about,"* that was what Dr. Waldo called it. Janie heard him tell Grams so. *Well, it simply wasn't true!* The way Janie figured it—Uncle Ted was getting on in the years. The old sawbones was out-of-it and didn't know what he was talking about. Grown-ups are so stupid.

Afterwards, Grams took her shopping at Marshall Field's and to Schenkel's cafeteria for Janie's favorite lunch of fried chicken, mashed potatoes, and tapioca pudding. Janie liked that part best, when it was just her and Grams in the cafeteria. They always took the same booth, the one beside the aquarium where she could watch the fish and marvel at the deep-sea diver and the treasure chest.

Oh, if she could only be a deep-sea diver! Treading on the ocean bottom, thirty fathoms below; just think of the excitement, the adventure, deep down under . . . Janie peered through the thick quartzite portal of her diving helmet; her entire world reduced to a circular three-inch view. The only sound was her own hollow breathing, and the click, click, click of the regulator. Air bubbles streamed past her view plate. There in the murky depth, she could just make out the broken remnants of an ancient Spanish galleon. Her underwater lantern cast a glint on a treasure chest overflowing with jewels, pirate plunder, and pieces-of-eight. She tugged on the umbilical and dug her weighted boots into the soft sand—on the surface, the loyal tender continued to pump life-giving air and payed out more hose. The treasure chest was tantalizingly close. Janie dug her hands into a mountain of gold doubloons. She was rich! So intent was she on her prize, she didn't notice, in the darkness, the devil-fish, a hideous amorphous mass with eight deadly sucker-armed tendrils. The ancient kraken saw her first, its huge unblinking eyes accustomed to the darkness; its razor-sharp parrot beak snapped as the monster from the deep enveloped her in an inky cloud.

"Janie."

No answer.

"Janie!"

"Um, what is it Grams?" Janie blinked. She suddenly felt foolish, wallowing on the floor of Schenkel's cafeteria, wrestling with the tablecloth. The entire table service, food, gravy, and crockery lay spilled, strewn about. Janie sat in a forlorn heap, her dress soiled. Grams was mortified, indignant, and furious. Two well-meaning busboys scurried over to see the cause of the tumultuous calamity, only to be surprised to discover one very small eleven-year-old girl doing battle with the table linen.

"Oh, Janie, why must you do these things?"

"I'm sorry, Grams," Janie sobbed, "It was an accident."

"With you, it's always an accident! Oh, Janie, your new dress." Grams whisked Janie off to the ladies' room to clean up. The busboys shook their heads and snickered. Thrifty Grams left a two-dollar tip.

All during the long train ride home, Janie sat very small and very quiet, bewildered and ashamed. Her beautiful new dress was ruined. Although Janie did think the Rorschach chicken gravy stain, which besmirched her blue calico print dress, did rather look like a map of Africa . . . when she made the teensy-weensy mistake of suggesting this to Grams—her grandmother was not amused, she was furious.

"Janie—you and your foolish daydreaming! Dr. Waldo said you need to concentrate more, focus.

Whatever am I going to tell your mother?"

Janie remained obstreperous. Grams wasn't there. She didn't see the giant octopus. Janie's only regret was that she didn't grab one of those gold doubloons when she had the chance. She really could use twenty-five cents to go to the movies on Saturday. Janie sighed a deep-down-satisfied sigh. The trip downtown, the vaccination, the debacle at Schenkel's—it had all been worth it.

"Daddy!" Janie clambered onto her father's lap. Her latest issue of *True Crime* clutched in her hand. A monumental stack of artillery computations got scrunched, scattered in the process. Her father became exasperated; he pushed Janie away. He had no time for such foolishness.

"Janie! It's your bedtime. Paula, get the children to bed, please. Can't you see I'm working!"

"Go to bed!" Janie groused. That was Mom and Dad's solution to every problem. Grown-ups positively refused to recognize the monumental importance of a crisis. Take, for example, Nazi U-boats in the cove. If one required any further proof as to the way grown-ups mucked-up everything, one only had to listen to the nightly broadcast of Edward R. Murrow. Janie lay wide-eyed and white-cheeked on the living room floor, basking in the subtle glow of heterodyne radio tubes as Mr. Murrow, his full rich baritone, filled the room. He spoke earnestly about something called D-Day, Omaha Beach, Hitler, Churchill, and Eisenhower. Janie listened intently. She didn't quite understand everything Mr. Murrow said, but it all seemed so very important.

Holly J. scoffed. "It's all noth'n but a bunch of hooey-baloney, if you ask me. Especially that sneaky four-eyed Jap Tojo—he's the stupidest grown-up of all!"

"Good night Holly J., good night Wednesday." Seven-the-cat lay curled up at the foot of the bed. Janie punched her pillow, readjusted her blankets, but couldn't get comfortable; she lay wide awake, she had troubles. The hall clock downstairs struck eleven. Still, she couldn't get to sleep. Finally, after the longest time, she poked Holly J., snoring lightly beside her. "Holly J., are you asleep?"

"Mmm?"

Janie sat up on one elbow. "Do you think grown-ups really know what they're doing? . . . like the war 'n all?"

"Heck no, like I told you before, grown-ups are mostly all wet—you just can't trust 'em."

"All grown-ups?"

"Well, there are a few . . . smart ones, I mean."

"How will I know?"

"You'll know, now go to sleep."

Janie was late for school. All this was especially embarrassing because Janie was a big girl, eleven-years-old this month. Her father chastised her. Her awful younger brother, Sid, teased her. Mother, on the other hand, took a sterner, less sympathetic approach.

"Jane Elizabeth!"

Ut oh, she was in big trouble now. Janie always knew when she was in big trouble 'cos Mom started using two names. "Janie, if you can't get up on time—you can't go to the movies on Saturday, that's final."

This was a catastrophe! Mother didn't seem to realize the dire straits of intrepid adventurer Captain Midnight. Why, in last week's episode, Captain Midnight and the beautiful Princess Cassandra found themselves captured by the evil Zerg-the-

Nefarious, merciless leader of the Moon-Men-from-Mars. Janie absolutely, positively had to find out what happened next!

On Saturday morning, sure enough, Janie was being punished. She couldn't go to the movies or leave her room. *Mother is so unfair!* When Mother wasn't looking, she climbed out the window, scaled down the trellis, and met up with Wednesday and Holly J. The three friends snuck off to the matinee. Mother found out, of course, (Sid, the rat, tattled on her). Oh my, was Mother cross! She whupped the tar out of her and sent her to bed without supper.

Janie buried her face in her pillow. Her ego bruised, her bottom smarted. Boy, was she mad! Mostly on account of Sid the rat. The monumental sense of injustice alone made her so angry, Wednesday and Holly J. got off scot-free!

Grams came from Chicago that very same day. Hooray, Grams to the rescue! Grams' visits were always a great source of tension in the McConaughey house. Grams didn't approve of spanking. She didn't get on so well with her daughter-in-law. Grams was of the opinion that her granddaughter was a troubled child and what she needed was less harsh discipline and more understanding (the Schenkel's cafeteria debacle long since forgiven). Grams had what you might call this terrible habit of interfering. Daddy said Mother was incorrigible. He disparagingly called her one of those "New Deal Democrats," Janie didn't know for sure what that meant, but whatever it meant, if being a New Deal Democrat included milk and cookies, (especially when you'd been sent to bed without supper), then Janie was all in favor.

Grams knocked on Janie's door. In defiance of Paula's discipline, Grams brought her granddaughter some milk and cookies. While Janie munched fragrant molasses cookies, Grams brushed her hair.

"When I was a little girl, my mother used to brush my hair one-hundred times before bedtime. It helps you go to sleep."

Her grandmother said softly, "Such lovely hair, pity your mother cut it so short."

It wasn't Mother. It was Wednesday . . . Janie thought. She knew better than to upset Grams by mentioning one of her friends. Janie's hair was short, "bobbed," a consequence of another one of Wednesday's wild schemes, scissors, and some misguided aspiration to be a hairdresser.

Ever sympathetic to Janie's plight, Grams brought her a present all the way from Chicago. Janie's sorrow instantly turned to joy as she eagerly tore open the wrapper.

"What is it, Grams?"

"Your very own alarm clock, child."

"Jeepers Grams! What the heck do I need with a dumb ol'-alarm clock?" Janie's face betrayed her disappointment. Grams only smiled.

It was an especially noisy alarm clock, too. The old-fashioned kind with a clapper and two brass bells. Janie was less-than-thrilled. Nevertheless, she set her alarm clock a full hour before it was time to get up.

"Sweetheart, why don't you try sleeping with the blinds open and your bed facing the morning sun?" Grams suggested. Nothing seemed to work; it all amounted to the same. Janie was late for school.

"Janie! Get up! Janie, please . . . You'll be late for school. It's your first day." Paula stood at the bottom of the stairs, spatula in hand, eggs, grits, and oatmeal bubbling on the stove. "Gosh darn that girl!" Her daughter still did not come down. Oh, she was up all right, wasting time, diddling about, fooling around with one of her wretched imaginary friends. Paula Mc-Conaughey thought herself a kind and understanding parent, but she found herself increasingly frustrated, exasperated by her daughter's constant disobedience.

Paula was quite familiar with Janie's shenanigans and her menagerie of imaginary friends. Janie was an ordinary child, quite normal. The problem started when she was four years old. At first, everyone thought it was cute. Paula chose to pass it off as an immature childhood flight of fancy. Not anymore; as Janie grew older, her relationship with these invisible people grew more intense. Now it was anything but cute. These were real people. Paula knew them all. Which one was it this time? Wednesday, Holly J., Seven-the-cat? 5, oh she hoped it wasn't 5. 5 was the worst, 5 was the troublemaker!

Dr. Waldo assured her it was just a "phase," he prescribed *Dr. Morse's Indian root elixir,* a particularly vile concoction of medicinal herbs, cocaine, and alcohol. Paula knew better. The patent medicine was no help, and this was no phase. Janie had this way of dragging you in—enmeshing you in her fantasies where sometimes Paula regarded these aberrations less as imaginary friends and more as annoying relatives who simply would not go home.

Originally, Paula hoped the move to Hartford would be good for the family, a fresh start in a new town, a new house, and a new school. Once again, Janie's ever-growing cast of characters reared its ugly head. What she once regarded as a mere fantastic fantasy now amounted to a constant headache. Over the years, Paula watched helplessly as her daughter slowly slipped away, an inexorable descent into the depths of madness the likes of which she was powerless to comprehend.

Her husband, Robert, was no help. Janie was his only daughter, and he doted on her shamelessly. A brilliant mathematician, and newly appointed Provost at Yale University, "Bob" was aloof, and utterly preoccupied with numbers, artillery tables, and the war effort. Robert McConaughey couldn't be bothered with such trivial matters.

"Deal with it, Paula, she'll grow out of it." was Robert's ever-present solution to the problem.

For political reasons, Robert viewed the family move from Chicago to Hartford as a catharsis, a chance for the family to begin fresh. Not to mention, when the President summons during wartime—one does not easily refuse the call. The university team at Yale was knee-deep in top-secret work: the frenetic development of a radio-controlled proximity-blast artillery fuse. There was nothing in the Axis arsenal to compare. Now an entirely new project landed on his desk; something called *Manhattan.*

Robert McConaughey was brilliant. The apple doesn't fall far from the tree, and all the McConaughey children were bright—Janie most of all. There was never any doubt that Janie was smart. In the fourth grade, Janie tested off the scale with an I.Q. of 168. That was half her problem. Janie was smart, too smart, smarter than all her classmates; fourth-grade arithmetic positively bored her. An idle mind is the "devil's workshop," and Janie was forever in cahoots with the devil. Janie was always first to finish her math assignment. She even finished her homework, and still she was bored. It wasn't her fault she had an over-active imagination.

Robert's ideal Janie was that of a fresh-faced, pig-tailed seven-year-old with two missing front teeth. Reality passed him by. He had no realization that his daughter was growing up. She was eleven-years-old, in the fifth grade, and forever lost in a fog of fantasy, preoccupied with a fantastic menagerie of people and places that didn't exist.

"Drink your orange juice, eat your toast."

"Mom!"

Sidney, Janie's eternally wretched, forever perfect, younger brother (who was only younger by thirteen months), was already spiffed, polished and out the door, along with eldest brother John, who was sixteen and in high school. Little Robert Jr., was just starting kindergarten.

"Oh, drat, that's the school bus, hurry up! Now let me look at you."

Janie stood for inspection in her blue-checked jumper crisply ironed, (besmirched with only a spattering of crumbs), fresh ribbons in her hair. White knee socks, one black saddle shoe (mostly) polished, the other only slightly smudged. Mother frowned, oh well, it would have to do. Mother kissed her forehead.

"I love you, darling."

"I love you, Mom . . . Mom!"

Paula sighed. There would be no peace until she complied, "Good-bye, Wednesday; good-bye, Holly J.; Janie, your school books!" Janie grabbed her book strap and beckoned her friends to follow.

Seven-the-Cat mewed. "No, Seven, stay home!"

"Janie, don't!" A pained expression crossed Paula's face. Janie slammed the door and skipped off the front porch to catch the school bus.

* * *

"Robert . . . it's your wife."

Robert McConaughey sighed an exasperated, over-burdened, what-is-it-this-time sort of sigh. He shoved aside his slide-rule, pencils, and stacks of computations. He grimaced, one-part embarrassment, two parts pure frustration. He glanced at his watch. Well, at least it was a full half-hour past the time of the usual panicked phone calls. Robert knew exactly what the call was about. Of his four children, John, Sidney, Robert Jr., and Jane—it was forever about Janie.

"Paula! Please, I'm in a meeting. Deal with it, don't you know there's a war on? When I come home, I promise you . . . when I come home, I'll deal with Janie."

"When ** w**ill ****tha*t ***be Bob?" Paula's voice crackled on the other line.

"What? Paula, I can't hear you." Despite the scant twenty miles between Hartford and New Haven, the long-distance connection was very bad. "On Friday, I'll be home on Friday. In the meantime, please, no more interruptions. Just get her to school."

* * *

Janie knew her father was important. President Roosevelt personally involved himself in the Congressional selection committee, which appointed Robert McConaughey Provost of the prestigious mathematics department at Yale University. The decision to give up his post at the University of Chicago, to uproot his family and move to small-town Hartford was an easy one. Robert personally selected Hartford as the new family home, the deliberate distance from New Haven served as an insulating factor. Robert viewed the new town, the new home as a necessity for a fresh start, a chance to begin with a clean slate, to leave behind the mountain of school referrals, police reports, and irate neighbors with their scurrilous, puerile complaints.

Robert was in denial. He found it impossible to believe that one very small eleven-year-old girl could possibly create such chaos. Janie climbed the roof of the Masonic temple (naked); Janie broke the lock and let all the animals loose at the Safeway pet store; Janie punched Mary Halberstadt, not because she was a Jew, but because Mary was a bitch and needed punching; Janie set fire to Mr. Raymond's shed (this was, in fact, the one thing Janie didn't do). It was those awful Mannock children from next door, Willie, Sharon, and Francis. Alas, because Janie ran with the wrong crowd, because of her past propensity for trouble, Janie took the blame just the same. Janie, it was forever about Janie.

On an intellectual level, Robert refused to admit that there was anything wrong with his daughter. Even though it was plain to everyone around him, her teachers, her doctor, and his wife—that Janie was an out-of-control, one-girl-wrecking-crew.

In many ways, Robert and Janie were more alike than comfort cared to admit. Robert remained utterly preoccupied, detached. When Robert came home from New Haven on Friday night, the ritual was always the same. Whiskey and soda, his pipe, and *Herald-Tribune.* Janie brought him his slippers. Supper was on the table promptly at six o'clock. Robert McConaughey spent the rest of the evening listening to Edward R. Murrow with his map, magnifying glass, and pushpins, charting the progress of Patton and Montgomery in North Africa.

* * *

Janie never intended to miss the school bus, honest. She walked to the bus stop, swinging her Dale Evans lunch pail, and her leather strap-bound school books. She waited with her baby brother Robert Jr. and her awful younger brother Sid. Janie made small talk with Maude, little Eleanor, and one of the eighth-grade girls, Crissy Greene. Like so many things that happened to Janie, it just happened. Waiting for the bus started out innocuously enough, then all-of-a-sudden there was trouble. One of the buckles on her shoe came loose. Janie tried, but she couldn't get her shoe to buckle. She fretted, fussed, and finally sat down on the curb in despair.

"5 will fix." 5 sat on its haunches, partially concealed in the bushes, its pale yellow-green eyes transfixed on the shoe.

"Go away, 5!" Of course, 5 didn't go away. As usual, 5 only made things worse. Which is not surprising, considering, what did 5 know about shoes? The thing didn't even wear clothes. Before Janie could stop it—feral 5 snatched the shoe. The number growled, tugged, and worried the buckle in its sharp teeth.

"Phooey, now the strap broke! What the heck am I gonna tell Mom?"

"Tell the bitch the strap was defective," 5 hissed, and slunk off into the shadows.

Tears welled in Janie's eyes. She was in big trouble and was in for a spanking! Shoes cost precious ration coupons. "Mom is gonna blow a gasket!" She could hear her mother screaming.

"Janie, what have you done! Don't you know there's a war on?"

The next thing Janie knew, she was alone, sitting on the curb. Grown-ups passed her by, briskly going about their grown-up business. From a child's eye view, Janie could scarcely make out their faces. Not that it mattered; busy grown-ups could hardly concern themselves with the plight of one very small eleven-year-old girl and one shoe that wouldn't buckle. *I'll just walk to school,* Janie thought. Suddenly, the once-familiar streets seemed strange and foreboding. Janie realized she didn't quite know the way to Charter Oak Grammar School. No worries, after all, how hard could it be?

Charter Oak was the name of Janie's school, a hallowed name known to every boy and girl in Hartford. The Charter Oak was this enormous white oak tree. According to tradition, in 1662, the Connecticut Royal Charter was hidden in the hollow of the tree. Blown down in a storm in 1812, this most noble of all oaks suffered an ignominious fate: the trunk was chopped up to make a chair.

Of course, none of this helped Janie find her way to school. So she struck out in the direction of Pleasant Street, past the newsstand owned by Mr. Hooper, the A&P grocery where Mother shopped. She stopped to pick up some green stamps dropped by a careless shopper. Janie figured she must have walked Pleasant Street hundreds of times; if you follow Pleasant, eventually you end up downtown on the corner of Market and Morgan. Janie looked right and looked left; there was Lang's drugstore and the Capitol theater where she went every Saturday afternoon to watch the *Captain Midnight* serials.

The day was sunny and the breeze fresh, it was a fine morning for a walk. The streets were lined with ancient oaks, the houses were neat and trimmed. Janie walked past a house with one of those iron "lawn jockeys," the little colored man hitching post, one Jocko Graves, a black youth who served General George Washington at the time he crossed the Delaware. Janie wished she was with George Washington, crossing the Delaware.

Janie tripped over the milkman.

"Hey, little girl, watch where you're going!"

"Sorry, mister." Janie skipped her way to school. Most houses had picket fences. She ran a stick across the slats as she walked. Some of the more affluent homes were appointed with an iron-railed fence; this diversion made a particularly grand racket. Janie noticed almost every house had one of those little flags with a blue star in the front window. Some had more than one, those homes had a son, or father serving in the armed forces, off somewhere in Europe fighting Hitler. There were gold stars, too.

"That means somebody got killed," Janie said.

Janie adjusted her pith helmet and foraged through the jungle underbrush. She slid down the mossy bank and found herself at the river's edge. She hid her school books, Dale Evans dinner pail, and took off her shoes and socks; she wouldn't be needing them, anyway. Janie beckoned to Wednesday and Holly J. and the three girls climbed into the canoe. The river was alive, teeming with hippos, crocodiles, and schools of deadly piranha.

"What about lunch?" Wednesday objected to leaving the dinner pail behind.

"We'll be back long before then," Holly J. said.

"I dunno, I'm kinda hungry now." Wednesday's stomach growled. She was always hungry and saw no good reason to leave behind a perfectly good peanut butter sandwich.

"Too much baggage," Holly J. bossed.

"So where are we going anyway?" Wednesday asked.

"To find the source of the Nile."

"Do you think we'll come across any wild animals?" Wednesday suddenly didn't feel so brave.

"Nothing much I should think, just lions and tigers and crocodiles," Holly J. said matter-of-factly. It was in this tense moment, the three friends heard a rustling in the bushes. A pair of yellow-green eyes lurked bright, something big and misshapen stalked the underbrush.

"Oh, my god!" Wednesday shrieked, "Eek, a crocodile!"

"Pshaw! It's only 5," Holly J. said with a sense of relief and annoyance. "It must have followed us here."

"Go away, 5!" Janie said. 5 snarled and gnashed its sharp teeth, unwelcome and unwanted, it reluctantly slunk away into the dense foliage.

The three friends paddled to the edge of the forbidden jungle. Before them lay a great vista of steamy rainforest and misty shrouded mountains. It was the age of discovery; the whole of an undiscovered continent lay before them. In that moment, all the discoveries of Columbus, Ponce de León, and Magellan seemed trivial by comparison. Janie, Wednesday, and Holly J. were poised to discover not just the source of the Nile, but judging from the sound of it, the source of all water on planet earth. Wednesday consulted the treasure map, the gravy-stained portion of Janie's Sunday dress.

"Where'd you get that?" Janie asked, horrified.

"Oh, I cut it out with some scissors."

There was mist in the air, the ground rumbled underneath their feet. There on the banks of the White Nile lay the forbidden secrets of the ancients and the realm of the Snapping Turtle God. Janie hacked at the dense vegetation with her machete. She swatted mosquitoes and intrepidly slogged into the unknown, and the deepest, darkest reaches of Africa, ruled by vipers and savage black cannibals.

Janie peeked over the rise. "Oh, crud!" The whole expedition turned out to be one colossal bust. There was no sacrificial altar, no blood, no pagan worship site, worst of all, no savage cannibals and their infernal boiling pot. Neither was any sign of Sir Richard Francis Burton, cartographer and explorer extraordinaire. Nope, none of that, nothing at all but the crummy Connecticut municipal hydroelectric dam spillway.

"Come'on you guys, let's go, there's noth'n to see here but rocks. Janie's gone 'n led us on another wild goose chase," Holly J. announced.

"Hey! I thought we came here to find the Temple of the Turtle Gods?" Wednesday became impatient. "Anybody got anything to eat? I'm starving! Some fine, fat, big-time explorers you all turned out to be. Stupid Janie left behind all our provisions!"

"Quit complaining, we'll forage for food. We're explorers. We'll eat moss, bugs, grubs, and junk." Forever the expert, Holly J. was insufferable. Janie didn't say anything, although as the sun pushed on to eleven o'clock, her tummy began to rumble. The prospect of eating bugs and grubs for survival loomed large, and she began to regret the decision to leave behind the dinner pail. The three friends pressed onward, descending into the depth of the pit. There was just a trickle of water in the culvert. It was all so disappointing.

"Wait." Janie flicked her Ronson lighter. *Lights up the first time, every time!* The lighter was a present from her Uncle Bud. Paula's brother was a tank commander somewhere in France, fighting Nazis. The lighter cast a flickery, eerie glow. Wednesday and Holly J. were eager to press on. Janie emerged from the culvert; the trickle of cool water on her bare feet became a stream, then a torrent. A light, misty, thunderous roar greeted her at the end of the tunnel. A lone girl picked her way across the concrete expanse of the Gothic-inspired balustrade, oblivious to any danger posed by the rapid discharge of three million gallons of water from the classic side-flow weir.

Janie Firefly, jungle explorer, felt very satisfied. Not only had she discovered the source of the Nile, but from the look of things, all water on the continent of Africa flowed from this source. Janie took two steps forward; the rushing cataract was considerably colder and deeper than she anticipated. The swift current knocked the girl off her feet and threatened to sweep her into the maw of the whirlpool below.

"Oh, crud! Help!"

Wednesday, who was bold as a dozen bears, and Holly J., who yanked tigers by their tails—not even wicked 5 came to her rescue. Janie bobbed to the surface; she choked and clutched.

"Halloo, Tochter!"

The native people who populated this region of Africa certainly turned out to be a distinct disappointment. Janie was expecting fearsome spear-wielding Maasai warriors with fantastic feather plumage and perhaps a token bone-through-the-nose. What she got instead was coveralls, work boots, and for some strange reason, the natives in these parts of Africa wore the exact same white helmets worn by Connecticut Con-Edison workers.

"Come on Kit, get on up out of there. You're going to get yourself killed!"

Jim reached down and, with a strong arm and a bit of luck, fished out one very small, very wet little girl from the rushing water. He held up the girl, choking and sputtering, like a prized trout. The kid was lucky to be alive. Two more seconds and the hapless child would have found herself swept into the turbine house. Jim Paradise shook his head. He was getting too old for this.

Jim Paradise retired to Hartford seeking a quite small-town life. He bought a house and applied for a job at Consolidated Edison. The day after the Japs bombed Pearl Harbor,

Jim promptly volunteered for civil defense duty. He was a retired police officer and was duly appointed chief civil defense officer of the City of Hartford. On paper, Paradise was beyond reproach. In hindsight, the city selectmen seemed to have overlooked the man they chose for the job was not an American, but German, a class C alien.

He was born Jakob Manfred Parajis in Dresden, Germany, in 1890. He came to this country when he was in his twenties. His parents were wealthy, educated, his father a university professor of music, his mother a grammar school teacher. For the past thirty-two years, Jim Paradise called America his home. He married, raised a family, grandchildren. He weathered the Great War and became a police officer, a detective, and arson investigator for the City of Queens. Now his world was torn apart by war. The Fatherland, his homeland, was once again at war with the world. Jim was a loyal American. Herr Hitler was no friend of his.

Janie had no idea as to her proximity to peril. What she did know was she was interrupted at the exact moment she was about to discover the source of the Nile. The sheer noise alone caused her not to hear the warning shouts from the man wearing the white CD helmet. The force of the water instantly swept the unlucky child off her feet. The water was ice-cold, freezing, so cold it sucked her breath away. Never in her life had Janie known such terror, such foolishness. The girl gasped, gulped, and choked. She looked up at the man who had saved her life. His face was wise and kind and full of years.

The old man chuckled as Janie coughed and sputtered. "Ach! Why you're noth'n but a tadpole, much too small for the keeping. Me thinks I shall throw you back." Jim facetiously pretended as if he fully intended to toss the poor hapless girl back into the cold rushing torrent.

Janie panicked. "Oh, no, please!"

"Dry land more to your liking, no?" Janie sputtered, shivered, and shook, just glad to be out of the rushing icy water. "Telling me now fräulein, what is your name?"

"Janie … Janie Firefly."

The old man considered this for a moment. "That's a very unusual name. I've not heard of very many Janie Fireflies, this is New England, no? It seems such a very special, fanciful name for such a small, ordinary American girl. Telling me Janie Firefly, what is your real name, eh?"

Janie crinkled her nose. "I don't like my real name."

"Really, why not?"

"Oh, I don't know, it's so very ordinary."

"Alright, Kit, let's try this a different way. Janie Firefly, pleased to making your acquaintance." Janie remembered her manners and shook hands with the old man. "My name is very ordinary indeed, my name is Jakob Parajis, but all my friends calling me Jim Paradise. Would you like to calling me Mr. Jim?"

Janie fidgeted, finally she said in a small voice, "Well, sir, I don't know you very well, and my daddy says I'm not supposed to talk to strangers. I don't suppose you know the way to Charter Oak Grammar School? I think I'm late."

Jim's smile betrayed his dissonance; he was taken aback. Although his motives were altruistic, he suddenly felt less like a rescuer and more like a predator. After thirty years on the police force, he'd had a belly full of bad men. The girl was right to be cautious. "Your father is right, of course, now that you're safe. I shall leaving you now to the schooling."

Wet, bedraggled, and more than a little bit pathetic, the prospects of sudden abandonment caused Janie to panic. "Oh, please sir, can't you stay just a little while longer? My daddy says I shouldn't call grown-ups by their first names. Now that we're introduced, I guess that doesn't make us strangers anymore. May I call you Mr. Paradise?"

"Mister Paradise will do just fine, but telling me Janie Fire-fly, what's calling you your real name?"

Janie grinned sheepishly. She finally felt enough at ease to tell Mr. Paradise her real name. "Janie McConaughey."

"Janie McConaughey," Jim said thoughtfully, "That's a nice name. Come Janie, I thinks I having a blanket in the truck."

"*Shht*, don't be a creep, don't tell him nothing, can't you see he's a Nazi!" Holly J. hissed. "Name, rank, and serial number, remember?"

Paradise frowned. The girl certainly was peculiar. He fetched the blanket, and the girl clutched its warmth. "Telling me fräulein, just who are you talking to?" After thirty years of police work, he'd seen some strange characters, but this girl was something altogether different. There was something decidedly curious about her. He was amazed to watch as she appeared to hold complete conversations with people who didn't exist—a one-girl-stage-play, where she played all the parts.

Janie gulped; finally, she found her voice, stood up, and looked straight at the man who called himself Jim Paradise. "Mister, are you from the U-Boat?"

"U-Boat? Around here, in Hartford?" The old man's eyes twinkled. At first, he thought it a caprice of whimsy, a foolish child's flight of fancy. Jim soon realized the little girl was earnest. There was something stark and serious about her, and her wild accusations were no joke. "Telling me fräulein, whoever, whatever, put this idea in your head?"

"Holly J. said . . ."

"Never mind, who is this Holly J.? Fräulein, telling me, what do you think?"

Janie looked Mr. Paradise square in the face, and with a worldly assuredness that belied her years, she firmly made her accusation: "I think you're a kraut, a heinie, and a hun! Mister, are you a Nazi spy?"

Paradise smiled faintly. The sheer absurdity of the child's accusation hit him in the gut. Then he laughed uproariously. "Is that it? Is that's what's bothering you mädchen? Nein, fräulein, I am an American."

"Really? Oh, wow! 'Cos on account Holly J. said . . ." Janie seemed genuinely relieved. "I thought for sure you was a Nazi saboteur! Me 'n my friends, Holly J., and Wednesday, we was exploring the Nile, in search of the realm of the Snapping Turtle God. We figured this was as good a place as any to find Jack Rackham, the Pirate King. Him and Wilhelm Manheim, the U-Boat Captain, this is where they was hiding out. They got Sir Richard Francis Burton held captive. I think they're holding him for ransom. Well, if you're not a Nazi spy, I guess that's okay. Mr. Paradise, does this mean I'm late for school?"

Jim concealed a snicker; the child was a wonder. "Jawol, fräulein, you are late for the schooling." Jim Paradise loaded one wet, bedraggled Janie Firefly into his big Model A Ford pickup and drove her the ten blocks to Charter Oak Grammar School.

"Auf Wiedersehen."

"Off what?"

"Good-bye, fräulein." Mr. Paradise waved and drove off.

At a quarter-past-eleven o'clock, Janie entered classroom no. 4, wet, sodden, and barefoot. Her beautiful blue-checked calico dress, torn and spattered with mud. Janie sidled over to her assigned seat, hoping no one would notice. Everyone noticed. Mostly, on account, with every step she took, she squished, scrunched, and smelled of swamp water. There rose a collective snicker from her classmates. *Crazy Janie McConaughey was late for school.* Miss Knich, her fifth-grade teacher, was not sympathetic. She peered sternly over the tops of her reading glasses; the little chain around her neck jiggled, and not in a good way.

Did she care?

She did not.

"Miss McConaughey . . . So good of you to join us. We were just about to begin arithmetic. Class, please open your math books to page 134." The chalk screeched on the blackboard. Miss Knich deliberately wrote in the corner, the one reserved for the names of naughty students: *M c C O N A U G H E Y.* Followed by the dread check mark.

"You're late!"

Chapter 2

Punch, Janie and Charlie

Robert McConaughey paid the cab driver and stealthily tip-toed up the driveway. He opened the screen door and slipped quietly through the kitchen, so as not to alert the family. Robert hated tumultuous reunions with almost as much ardor as his family looked joyously to his weekly homecomings. After a long week of managing facts, figures, and calculations, the last thing he wanted was to be besieged by four rambunctious children and his dear, long-suffering wife and her carryings-on of Janie's latest misbehavior.

Daddy was home! When supper dishes were cleared, when her homework was finished, the family settled in the living room. Her father in his favorite chair, Mother took up her crocheting, and Sidney was busy playing with his army men. Janie brought daddy his pipe and slippers. She curled up expectantly at his feet. This was the quiet time Janie liked best. Robert switched on the big RCA radio, sat back, and lit his pipe. Soon, the whole house was filled with the wonderful, familiar aromatic scent of tobacco.

"This is London. In the first days of June, 1944, just days after the great Allied invasion of Normandy, the Nazis unleash a new terror weapon, the V-1 flying bomb. Called Hitler's revenge weapon in retaliation for the Allied invasion, in continuing devastating attacks on London, the V-1 is a new kind of weapon—a terror weapon. Now armed with this new "secret weapon," Hitler proclaims Germany's victory inevitable. The V-1 cruise missile attacks on London have continued unrelenting ... when the worst was thought to be over, today Germany unleashed yet a new terror weapon, the V-2, a supersonic ballistic missile. The V-2 strikes without warning and is utterly unstoppable. Before signing off tonight, I want to leave the good people of London with this thought: No one can terrorize a whole nation unless we are all his accomplices. This is Edward R. Murrow reporting from London. Good night and Good Luck."

* * *

School was out, and Charles Reilly, or Charlie as he was called back then, couldn't remember a time when he was so glad to be out of school. The promise of summer vacation and all the glorious boyhood freedom to have all summer long with nothing to do—and all day long to do it. You might think turning thirteen, and graduating from the eighth grade in the summer of 1944, on the eve of the greatest invasion in history, might have felt more ominous. Not for Charlie. Storm clouds were looming; the world was at war. Two million Allied soldiers stood poised to storm the beaches of Normandy, but life on the home-front in Hartford, Connecticut, went on pretty much as it always had.

Charlie's father was Irish Catholic, his mother a strict Lutheran, no small wonder Charlie grew up a little bit confused. As the Reilly's only child, his parents had high expectations. His mother wanted him to be a doctor; his father, a lawyer.

Uncle Nelson promised him an apprenticeship in the family business. Charlie managed to disappoint them all. What did Charlie want to be? A comedian—Charlie was funny, very funny. Being funny was the one thing Charlie knew he was good at. He excelled at the art of telling a joke and possessed a droll sense of humor, and he loved making people laugh. Charlie, along with B.D. (Beady) Bronson, his acerbic wise-cracking ventriloquist dummy, were the perennial hit of bar mitzvahs, birthday parties, and family gatherings all over Hartford.

Charlie wasn't like other boys; he wasn't good at sports like Ronnie-Ray, or smart as Richard Vanderbilt. Charlie was a shy, gawky boy with big glasses and an even bigger secret: Charlie was *different.* Charlie was different at a time when being different was just about the worst possible thing a boy could be. Charlie wasn't confused. He was pretty sure of himself. It was just that for as long as he could remember, he didn't like girls. No sir, didn't like 'em, didn't even find them attractive. Ooh, how he hated that snooty Crissy Greene in her frilly, flowery girly dress, her perfectly beautiful coiffed blonde curls, and her huge *you-know-whats.* Charlie spent more than a few furtive hours fantasizing about Charles Atlas, Johnny Weissmuller, and Jack Armstrong than he ever did about any dumb ol' girl.

Charlie was smart enough to know that sometimes it was best to keep the fact that you were different to yourself; there were plenty of people ready, willing, and able to beat the crap out of you just for being different. For now, Charlie kept his secret and contented himself with his comedy, his jokes, and his puppet shows.

What Charlie worried about most was what his mother would think. Well, there was no sense worrying about that, he knew what Mother would think. She'd scream and holler and chase him around the kitchen with a wooden spoon.

"Charlie, you were raised better than that!"

His father, on the other hand, that was his worst fear. Charlie was quite certain if the old man ever found out—he'd stroke dead away.

"Somebody get the smelling salts!" Aunt Zetti always overreacted to everything. Charlie's favorite aunt rushed into the parlor where her brother lay collapsed on the floor. "Charles, can you hear me? Oh, my back! Charlie, fetch a shot of brandy!" Aunt Zetti downed the liquor in one gulp and continued to fan her poor faint brother, overcome with grief and shame.

"Holy fudge, what a scene!"

The worst thing that ever happened was at missionary meeting where Charlie was asked to perform a puppet show. When the time came for him to be introduced, Mrs. Begley, well-meaning, sweet Mrs. Begley, got up in front of the Father Carpenter and the whole parish and called him: "That funny little boy with big glasses who liked dolls." The careless remark left Charlie feeling dismal and alone.

No, come to think of it, that wasn't the worst. The absolute worst was the day when Mr. Clark, the gym teacher, ushered all the boys into the auditorium. Charlie knew something was up, and what was up was no good.

"Men, I don't want to hear any laughing or snickering." There in the darkened auditorium, Charlie was subjected to a particularly grueling form of academia. Welcome to hell—welcome to Health Class. Charlie was forced to watch a perfectly awful filmstrip: *Your Body and You.* Complete with a record player that went "ding" when the time came to change the frame. The monotonous monotone voice intoned ad nauseam a clinical dissertation on what goes where and why.

"Hey Charlie, maybe now you'll score with Crissy Greene!" Charlie felt a wad of paper smack the back of his head. Charlie was humiliated; he hated girls. Girls were repulsive, girls were gross. No sir, he didn't like 'em.

Much to Charlie's surprise, he was about to discover his new best friend, his only friend, the one person in all-the-world who did not judge him, who accepted him, who truly believed in him—was the strangest person of all. She was a girl.

* * *

"What-cha' all doing? Can I play?" Janie asked with an air of innocence and lack of worldly sophistication that belied her ten-years-old going-on-eleven. Charlie whirled around, shocked, caught off guard in a sudden flurry of forbidden activity. There he was, surrounded by all his puppets, mostly a collection of sock puppets, papier mâché, and one ventriloquism dummy, B.D. Bronson. Nobody, absolutely nobody, appreciated, let alone understood him or his puppets.

"Nothing, now go away!"

"Sure, don't look like nothing to me."

Charlie rolled his eyes. Just his luck. Jane McConaughey was the absolute worst! Not only the creepiest girl in the fifth grade, she was the creepiest girl in all of Connecticut. Charlie groaned. *Why me?* There simply wasn't a queerer three-dollar bill in all of Hartford than Jane McConaughey!

"Can I help? I can color."

"I said scram!" Janie didn't scram. She stood there, smiling expectantly. Charlie looked up. *Who was he kidding?* He really could use some help. Between the scenery, backdrops, and props and puppets, it was all too much for one person. Janie took an orange crayon and meticulously began to color. Charlie watched her critically, but true to her word, the girl really could color. Good! Now maybe she could finish the scenery while he returned to the tedious task of sewing the eyes on his sock puppets. Janie finished one scene and was working on the second. Charlie felt like he was really making progress. That was until Janie began an animated argument (with herself).

"Ah, applesauce! What the heck is the matter now?" Charlie peered over the tops of his glasses, dismayed. He watched the goofy girl assail a non-existent person in a heated argument.

"It's 5 . . ."

"Who?"

"5 stole all the orange crayons and won't give them back!"

"Who's five?"

"It's 5. 5 is not a who—5 is a number. Besides, you don't want to know anyways." Janie was adamant, she added under her breath, less as an afterthought and more as a warning, "On account 'cos 5 does bad things."

Charlie grimaced. He felt intractably sucked into Janie's world and her game of invisible, imaginary people. Okay, he'd play along. "Why not?" Charlie demanded.

"Oops, I think 5 ate them." Janie smiled coyly.

To his horror, Charlie could plainly see the girl from next door—her teeth covered in bright orange crayon. "Jane! You dumb Dora! Spit that out. You ain't got no more brains than a piss-ant. Now you've gone and spoiled everything." Charlie fumed, "I knew I never should have trusted you. Now, I don't have enough crayons to finish the scenery." Charlie was in big trouble. What if the creepy neighbor girl somehow managed to poison herself? And with his crayons!

Janie smiled sweetly.

"Beat it, Jane, you're too weird!"

"My name is Janie, Jane Elizabeth—Jane 'E' get it?" Janie put on a pout. A boy who sews his own doll clothes just called *her* weird. "It wasn't my fault! Blame 5 . . ." Janie continued to smile a particularly orangey smile. Without missing a beat, she asked, "Chucky, what's the name of this dumb ol' puppet show anyways?"

"La Traviata," Charlie said proudly. His love for opera and his excitement over the puppet show caused him momentarily

to forget the crayon catastrophe. This was going to be his best play ever. "It's an opera."

"Oh, is that sumpt'n like singing 'n stuff?" Janie asked, "'Cos I think you got a word spelled wrong, C O U R T I S O N. Shouldn't that be spelled C O U R T E S A N? Chucky, what's a courtesan?"

"Janie, how can you be so stupid? And don't call me Chucky! How come you know how to spell a word like courtesan and you don't even know what one is?"

"Jeepers, Chucky," Janie shrugged her shoulders and resumed coloring. "I dunno, I just know how to spell stuff, that's all."

Charlie was clearly uncomfortable. He fidgeted, acted embarrassed, and finally said in a hoarse whisper, "A hooker."

"A what?" Janie frowned.

"A lady of the evening, a prostitute, tramp, tart, a whore. Okay, I've gone and said it—I hope you're satisfied!"

Janie thought for a moment, "Oh, is that all. Chucky, is this gonna be a dirty play? 'Cos if it is, my mother would be powerful provoked with me if she knew I was help'n out on a dirty play. We're Methodist."

Charles wiped his glasses nervously, "Of course not, it's French!"

"Chucky, do you want me to finish coloring these palm trees? You got any more orange crayons?"

* * *

The house on 625 Elm was a modest dwelling, common for the area, a typical nineteenth-century New England "saltbox" farmhouse. The house was so perfectly ordinary in its appointments that at first Janie was disappointed. This couldn't be the place. She'd imagined him living in a much bigger house, a grandiose Tara, a mansion set high on the bluff with pillars, turrets, and hedgerows, resplendent with verdant grounds impeccably manicured, complete with leafy topiary, heroic equestrian statuary, and a fantastic, fantasy fountain squirting water. Nope, none of that. Instead, all she found was a regular ol' clapboard house with a white picket fence and some crummy rose bushes.

Janie sat down on the curb, took off her skates, and ran up the driveway.

Jim Paradise was working in his garage. He hunched over the motor of his Ford truck, intently twiddling, fiddling with the starter. *You've seen better days, my old friend.* His wrench slipped. The rusty bolt creaked and broke with an audible snap.

"Gottverdammmt!" Now he'd have to use the torch. He remained blissfully unaware of the little blonde girl stealing up the drive behind him. She shouted in his ear.

"Helloo, Mr. Paradise!"

Jim was startled; he reared up and smacked his head square on the hood of the truck, hard enough he saw stars. He turned around, rubbing his poor head. He was greeted by the smiling, cherubic, dimpled cheeks of Janie McConaughey.

Paradise held his head, "Ach, Tochter! I wish you wouldn't do that!"

"Aren't you glad to see me, Mr. Paradise?"

Jim wiped his hands on a rag. His worn face concealed a bemused grin; he could hardly be angry with the child. She certainly did possess a certain ebullient enthusiasm that was difficult to dismiss. Still, there was cause for concern. *Had the child run away again?* Jim didn't really know her well enough to be worried, but one thing he'd figured out for sure. The girl was a teufel.

"Telling me Kit, how on earth did you find me?"

"Oh, that was easy," Janie laughed, "I called the operator, Mrs. Parker. She gave me your name, address 'n everything, Chapel 4-5419."

"Janie Firefly, you are quite the little detective." Jim Paradise was amazed; he'd spent a career suffering dummkopf junior detectives who were not half so resourceful. "Well, Janie, now that you're here, what brings you to visit Mr. Paradise today?"

"Oh, nothing, I just wanted to see you again. What 'cha doing? Is your truck broke? Can I help? . . . Me and Wednesday, we're very good at fixing things."

This wasn't exactly true; Wednesday wasn't mechanical in the least. She was so bad, in fact, Janie liked to joke that Wednesday couldn't fix anything with more moving parts than a bowling ball. The child was quick and before Jim could stop her, Janie up-ended the tray containing all the washers, nuts, and bolts from the disassembled starter. Jim was a patient man. He didn't chastise her. He allowed himself an agonized grimace as dozens of minuscule parts flew into the air in slow motion and scattered to oblivion.

"Golly, Mr. Paradise, those parts sure are small, huh? Want me to help you look for 'em?"

"Nein fräulein, you've done enough." Jim took the mischievous child by the hand and led her away before she could wreck his entire garage. "Mr. Paradise having a better idea. What do you say we go inside; I think I might having some milk and the strudel. You like something sweet for the sweet, no?"

"What's that, Mr. Paradise?"

"Strudel?"

"No, in your belt."

A momentary flash of irritation crossed Paradise's face. "Ach! Nothing for very jung mädchens to be concerning themselves!" Jim was immediately sorry for speaking crossly to the girl. She was naturally precocious. She'd meant no harm. Jim knew exactly what piqued the child's curiosity. Tucked in his waistband was a *Pistole Parabellum,* a Luger pistol.

"Mmm, this strudel sure is good. Did you make it, Mr. Paradise?"

"Nein, mein housekeeper, Frau Detweiler, she making the strudel."

"Oh, boy, please tell Mrs. Detweiler this strudel sure is good!" Janie held her spoon down low to the floor. Seven-the-cat lapped the spoon. "I don't think Seven ever had such good strudel before." Frau Detweiler frowned and fretted from behind the sanctuary of the kitchen door, as spoonfuls of syrupy, spicy, appley goodness dripped on her impeccably clean floor.

Janie continued to scoop heaping spoonfuls of crisp apple pastry; she took a cold, satisfying drink of sweet milk. Whole milk, too, at home her mother watered down the milk to make it stretch further.

"Mr. Paradise, are you rich?"

Jim smiled. "Not really fräulein, I live on a pension."

Janie's eyes took time to wander around the parlor. It was a nice room and smelled faintly of tobacco. A family photograph on the mantle caught her eye. A much younger Mr. Paradise, a woman, and three children, Janie got up to take a closer look.

"Is this your family, Mr. Paradise? Where's Mrs. Paradise?"

"Frau Paradise is passed away. Helga, she live in New York with her husband. Ernst and Fritz they go to university in Dresden. I receive a letter. They have joined the Wehmacht and are stationed somewhere in France, a place called Caen."

"Oh, I'm sorry about your wife, Mr. Paradise. I mean . . . pictures sure do tell a bunch. But that's real neat, about Ernst and Fritz. My Uncle Bud, he's in France too! Maybe they'll meet up."

Jim smiled faintly; *maybe they'll meet up.* Oh, child, how little you know about the world. The girl's innocence was sobering. This war, this terrible war, this all-consuming war, had a way of drawing everyone in, ordinary everyday common people, chewing them up and spitting them out like meat from a grinder. Tens of millions of innocent lives ruined by this wicked war. He thought of his own two sons, good honest boys, fighting in Europe for the Nazi cause. The thought was suddenly too painful, too personal for him to contemplate. He decided to change the subject. "Telling me fräulein, what brings you here to see Mr. Jim today?"

"Like I said, I just wanted to see you again, that's all. Mr. Paradise? Holly J. said you was a Nazi spy, but I just knew that wasn't true. I just wanted to thank you for what you done, you know, saving me 'n all. I shouldn't have done what I done, and I wouldn't have 'cept'n on account 5 busted the buckle on my shoe. I hid them in the bushes along with my Dale Evans lunch box. I lost my shoes and now Mother is powerful mad at me."

Tears flooded Janie's eyes. "I'm a bad kid. I know 'cos Mother says so. Mother says I'm foolish and careless, and I diddle about and there're no more ration coupons for new shoes. Now I gotta wear Sid's crummy boy shoes to school! Mr. Paradise, what am I going to do? I can't wear boy shoes to school! I think I'm going to die!"

"Is this why you coming to see me today, because of boy shoes?"

Janie sniffed. "No sir, I just wanted to thank you for saving my life. Wednesday, Holly J. 'n me, at first we was hunting for a Nazi U-boat and Jack Rackham, the Pirate King. Wednesday, she said as long as we was in Africa, we might as well search for the source of the Nile and the realm of the Snapping Turtle God. That's what I was do'n down by the river until I got lost and in a mess, and in case you really are a Nazi spy like Holly J. said. You don't have to worry. I'll never, ever tell 'cos you're a good man. You 'n me we're friends."

Jim listened patiently. Once she got started, the child was a chatter-box. "Telling me, Janie Firefly, this is what's troubling you? A lost pair of shoes?" Jim chuckled to himself, and here all along he thought it was something dire. "Frau, please bring my ration coupon book from the desk." Janie's eyes grew big as saucers.

In 1944, America was at war with the world. Every kid in America knew there were shortages of rubber, gasoline, and shoes. Ration coupons were more valuable than gold, not something to be given away lightly. Janie watched as Mr. Paradise tore from his ration book a coupon for one pair of new shoes. Jim looked down at his own worn boots. They were good enough.

"Janie Firefly, I want you to promise me, taking this coupon and give to your parents. They will buy you a new pair of shoes." Janie was so happy; her heart must have skipped a beat. She could hardly contain her excitement. Just think of it, new shoes! She threw her arms around the old man and kissed him on the cheek. It was a real wet kiss, too.

"Oh, Mr. Paradise, you're the best friend I ever had!" Jim smiled; she was a dear child, so much like his daughter, Helga, head in the clouds, her heart in the right place. *Ja, schätzchen, I love you, too.*

* * *

"Chucky, wait up!" Janie chased her friend down the long aisle of Quigley's hardware. Janie never knew such a wonderful place existed. Everywhere she looked, there was some new discovery. Shelves filled with nuts, bolts, and mechanical thing-a-ma-jigs. "You promised me a Nehi!" Charlie tossed Janie a ball of twine, some fine wire, hooks, screws, and a bag of junk used to make papier mâché. Quigley's hardware was an absolute goldmine, a Mecca for aspiring theater designers. The haul came to $1.68, and Charlie still had thirty-two cents left—Janie would get her Nehi.

Robert "Bobby" Dale Segee sat on the fence behind Quigley's hardware, smoking a cigarette. He sat there for a long time, not thinking much about nothing. After all, he had nothing better to do with his time. Sitt'n loose on a fence rail came easy for Bobby Segee, he could do it all afternoon long. Effortlessly, and all without a single erudite thought to trouble his addled brain. He was almost sixteen, but still in the eighth grade. One month shy of the legal drop-out age, not that it mattered. Bobby didn't go to school much these days, anyway; Bobby failed every grade, every subject since sixth grade. He was stupid. He knew he was stupid because his teachers told him so. He'd spent more than a few long hours sitting in the corner with a "dunce" hat on his head. Yeah, that about summed it up: Bobby Segee was just about as dim-witted as they come. Feckless as he was stupid, with a shiftless streak a mile wide. Abused and abandoned, the youngest of seven children, he was born on the wrong side of the blanket, the illegitimate son of a washer-woman and a drunkard father.

It wasn't as if his natural affection for laziness was all his fault. His pap, Jonas Segee, was renowned, positively legendary in five counties for two things: his penchant to pull a cork and his bone-idle laziness. Folks once said Jonas was so lazy, as he lay on the front porch, the parade passed by.

Ma came running out of the house. "Pa, the parade is passing by!"

"Durn it all, woman, can't you see I'm facing the wrong way?"

There was no denying he was Jonas Segee's son. They say you can recognize a bad egg without trying to lay one, and Bobby Segee sure as shoot'n was a bad egg. Bobby burnt down his family's home when he was seven. When he was twelve, he lured nine-year-old Barbara Driscoll down to the banks of the Piscataqua River. Segee later claimed they argued, that Barbara called him names. The facts are far more gruesome. There in the thick cattails beside the rushing riparian waters, he raped, strangled, and bashed her head in with a rock.

Bobby Segee sat on the fence rail eating an apple. He punctuated his idleness by periodically spitting out the seeds. He sat and waited with deliberate acrimony for Charlie Reilly to come out of Quigley's store. As dim-witted as he was, Bobby may not have known much, but the one thing he knew for sure was that Charles Sr., Charlie's father, was rich. It was well known around town that Mr. Reilly ran a successful business and his family enjoyed a highfalutin lifestyle. It was also no secret that Charlie received the unheard-of sum of seventy-five cents a week allowance. What a waste! Seventy-five cents sure could buy a lot of cigarettes and corn liquor.

Charlie and Janie tumbled off of the back porch of Quigley's store, laughing and jostling, flushed with success from their purchases. Their spirits were high, their talk was buoyed with excitement. Janie was especially excited because Charlie promised to take her to Lang's drugstore and treat her to a Nehi. Charlie was equally enthusiastic, eager to resume work on his puppet show. The two friends took no notice of the idle boy sitting on the rail fence.

One might pause to conjecture what wicked mischance of misfortune placed unassuming Charlie on a collision course with a calamitous cretin like Bobby Segee? That was the easy part; Charlie had the rotten luck of being in the same eighth-grade class. Charlie was at the top of his class, unlike the hulking Neanderthal Segee who'd flunked two grades. Bobby hated Charlie—Charlie played with dolls, Charlie had seventy-five cents, and he didn't. Worst of all,

Charlie was friends with the creepiest girl in the whole school, Janie McConaughey.

"Whoa! What's you gone 'n got there? Don't tell me the biggest pansy in the eighth grade finally went 'n got himself a girlfriend! And a young 'un too, what is she, about six?"

"Go away and leave us alone," Charlie said, with as much bravery as he could muster. "Com'on, Janie, let's go."

Charlie never planned to grab Janie's hand. It was an impulse, a fractious act of spontaneity. Hand-holding, especially holding a girl's hand, was not the usual sort of social interaction Charlie ever thought himself capable. Nevertheless, there he was, before he knew it—he and the McConaughey girl were clasped hand-in-hand. Less like sweethearts and more like a big brother desperately trying to make his little sister hurry up. Charlie grimaced, mistake number one. He just knew it was a mistake to take the shortcut behind Quigley's hardware, mistake number two.

Bobby hopped down off the rail fence and blocked their path. He made rude kissing sounds, as he hugged himself and taunted:

Janie and Charlie sittin' in a tree, K-I-S-S-I-N-G,
First comes love, then comes marriage,
then comes the baby in the baby carriage.
Suckin' his thumb, wettin' her pants,
doin' the naked nasty dance.
That's not all, that's not all, Daddy's drinking alcohol!

"You take that back!" Janie stuck out her tongue. "Bobby Segee is a bologna butt!"

"I oughta kick yer can fer that!"

Charlie did something that surprised even Charlie—he stepped between the bully and the impish girl.

"Gimme yer lunch money, faggot!"

"He can't get away with that. Sock him, Chucky!" Janie was fight'n mad. Even if she wasn't exactly sure what a "faggot" was, she was in no mood to stand around while some big ape called her friend nasty names.

Janie had no comprehension as to the intractable trouble she'd created. Charlie couldn't fight the big boy. Charlie told jokes, Charlie played the ukulele. Charlie was not a brawler, bruiser, or fighter. Naïve Janie regarded her friend in far more epoch terms. He was her Sir Lancelot, Beowulf, Gilgamesh.

"Chucky, what about the Valkyrie?"

"Don't be goofy, those are only operas."

"Oh, from what you said before about the Nibelungen, I thought Brünnhilde was supposed to swoop down and vanquish the oppressors. I remember you said, Brünnhilde is the champion of justice, our lady protector, and defender of the weak!"

"Utshay-upway upidstay . . ." Charlie said under his breath.

"Chucky, what's upidstay?"

"Janie, you're not helping," Charlie already felt ashamed—he wasn't a coward, it was just he could never be the dashing knight in shining armor Janie imagined. Charlie saw no other way out of his predicament. He sheepishly dug into his pocket and prepared to hand over the extortion money.

"You're not going to give him your money?" Janie was incredulous.

Segee was equally incensed. "That's it? Thirty-two fuck'n cents?" Segee chucked the apple core at Charlie's chest. "You'd better cough up more dough than that, and quick, you four-eyed-queer!"

Janie McConaughey was not so easily intimidated. The feisty girl clenched her jaw; the physical transformation that came across the eleven-year-old's face was stark and terrifying. Janie's demeanor became dark as a thunderhead storm cloud, her eyes narrowed to evil slits.

"One, two, three, all hell is about to break loose and that is me," Janie said in a voice that was not her own. "I'd watch it if I were you. 5 says it doesn't like you."

Neither Charlie nor Bobby had the slightest comprehension of the dire seriousness of Janie's warnings. 5 was evil, 5 was a loathsome, villainous primitive. If the girl said 5 was around—the real person in danger was Bobby Segee.

The hulking sixteen-year-old afforded Janie's threats all the gravitas of a chirping cricket. Segee cracked a shit-eating-grin; he had Charlie right where he wanted him. As for his creepy girlfriend, the talk around town was the McConaughey girl "heard voices," talked to people who didn't exist. Bobby Segee wasn't worried about any weirdo snot-nosed girl.

"You show are *ignert*." Bobby laughed in Janie's face and pushed the fifth-grader down. Janie landed on her butt without grace in the dust. "Go'n, git! Run home 'n play with yer dolls! I hear Charlie's got lots of dolls—maybe he'll let you play with some of his!"

Janie got up, dusted herself off, and smiled sweetly. She did not cry. If Bobby was expecting her to burst into tears and start bawling like a dumb, stupid girl, he was sorely disappointed.

"I said, 5 doesn't like you." Without warning—5 charged, hauled off, and kicked the big boy in the balls. Bobby was five years older, a foot taller, and a hundred pounds heavier. Size, weight, didn't matter—nothing mattered. 5 tore into Bobby with a baneful fury—it knocked him down and pinned the boy to the ground. 5 punched him, pummeled him, and savaged his face. Bobby shrieked, hollered "nuff," the traditional schoolyard plea of submission. The thing snarled, ignoring his pathetic pleas of surrender. Once unleashed, there was no mercy—5 was a remorseless, pitiless attacker.

Feral 5 closed its talons around the boy's throat. A pure sociopath, without feeling, without remorse—5 was intent on throttling the life out of Bobby Segee.

"Stop it, 5!" Janie screamed.

"5 thinks it will kill this boy." Janie's voice came from another world.

"No, 5, that's enough . . . please 5—Let him go!"

"5 will leave," 5 hissed. "Maybe next time . . ."

Bobby Segee choked and gasped for breath. The big bully held his bloody cheek where the crazy bitch bit him. He fled the vacant lot behind Quigley's store, bruised, bloodied, and blubbering like a little shoat pig.

"What the heck is the matter with you? Are you crazy?" Horrified by the sheer violence of the psychotic episode, Charlie pulled Janie off Bobby. The girl was still snarling. The savage entity that possessed his friend was finally gone. Its murderous fury spent, leaving Janie unconscious. Charlie checked to make sure she was still breathing. This couldn't be happening. Think, Charlie, think, this was worse than a disaster, this was a catastrophe! Charlie Reilly could see the headlines now:

CHARLES REILLY, EIGHTH-GRADER,
DEFENDED BY A GIRL
Eleven-year-old schoolgirl beats up local bully,
saves Charles Reilly!

Yeah, it all amounted to a public relations disaster for Charlie. His life was all but over—everyone, Aunt Zetti, Uncle Nelson, Father Carpenter—everyone will think this was hilarious. That was half the problem—they didn't see the murderous glint in the little girl's eye, hear her growl, or see her face come away bloody. What terrible demons tortured her soul? Charlie was sure he didn't know.

* * *

"Frau Detweiler, will you please bring me a book from the library? The medical book. I need to look up something. . . something on schizophrenia."

Chapter 3

Summer Daze

The Sherman tank rammed its boscage breaching "tusks" at the root base of the sixteen-foot-tall, centuries-old hedgerow. The 400 horsepower Chrysler engine roared and the tank's tracks churned. The stubbornly knotted roots of the shrubbery strained, then finally ripped and gave way as the 33-ton armored monster burst forth through the dense undergrowth, only to plunge once again down into a sunken lane of the French countryside.

"Driver, turn left!" It was D-Day plus five. Lieutenant Robert "Bud" Clayton shouted his commands from atop the cupola. The tank lurched; its treads ground the dirt and struggled to gain traction in the loamy soil. *This was not good tank country,* Bud thought. As far as the eye could see, well, in fact, there was nothing to see but a sunken road and these god-cursed hedgerows. The Germans could be anywhere, lurking, skulking. Bud was left with only one choice: keep moving forward.

Janie released the clutch and pushed the driving levers forward. In many ways, it was just like driving a car, except her entire world was reduced to the three-inch view afforded by her periscope. Janie glanced over to 5, metallic belts of ammunition clattered. Ever ready, 5 jerked back the charging lever on the bow machine gun. Its claws on the trigger, the thing was barely able to contain its glee at the prospects of machine-gunning some hapless Germans.

Up in the turret, loader Wednesday and gunner Holly J. waited for their commander's orders. The Sherman labored down the sunken lane; Bud scanned the horizon for the slightest movement. The tank was vulnerable. Bud's head poked out of the cupola. His radio set cocked, one ear on, one ear off. It was one of the occupational hazards of being a tank commander. One might think prudence dictates a safer course of action: hide behind the shield of the Sherman's thick armor. This, however, wasn't practical; you simply could not effectively command a tank buttoned up. The Germans were everywhere, wily, crafty, and ready for an ambush. Bud needed to be able to see what was going on.

Then it came.

Without warning, a German anti-tank gun cracked, the shell careened, crashed, and burst against the front glacis plate. The explosion was so violent it knocked the turret crew to the floor. When the smoke cleared, the Sherman survived. They build them well in America. Janie was temporarily blinded by the blast. Maniacal 5 cackled with delight and screamed obscenities. The bow machine gun chattered, spewing a vicious stream of white-hot lead in all directions.

"Fire!" Bud screamed. "Load HE, gunner traverse." Bud took temporary shelter behind the mantlet. He kicked Janie in the small of her back. This wasn't as rude as it seemed; in the heat of battle, voice commands were often lost or misunderstood. Tank commanders used foot commands to control their drivers: a foot on the right shoulder, turn right, left shoulder, turn left. Janie was blinded by the explosion; she pulled back on the driving-levers. The gearbox shrieked as she threw the tank in full reverse. The big Chrysler engine snorted, belched, and the tank began to retreat, still dragging half of a shrubbery caught in its tines.

"Fire!" Bud scanned the horizon with his powerful Zeiss binoculars. There was a glint in the thicket. There was no time, a second German shell slammed into the dirt in front of the tank. A white-hot shell splinter ricocheted off the Sherman's armor and pierced his shoulder. It knocked him down. Bud felt himself falling, failing as he collapsed into the turret's interior.

"The commander is hit!" Holly J. screamed.

"Gunner, traverse left, six degrees, fire!" Bud rasped. He was on his feet, bleeding profusely. He refused to relinquish command. It took all his strength to clamber back up into the commander's cupola. Now he was fighting mad. Bud jerked on the charging lever of the big .50 caliber machine gun. "Ma duce" was about to give the Germans something to think about!

"Thwbbbthhhhh . . ."

"Janie, what in Sam Hill do you think you're doing?" It was Sid, Janie's perfectly awful, bratty younger brother. "Mom is looking for you; the Sheriff is looking for you. They say you jumped Bobby Segee 'n beat him up bad. You're in big trouble! What the heck you do'n out here anyways?"

Janie looked down from her perch atop the rusted derelict hulk of the 1898 Case steam traction engine. The tractor sat long abandoned in the bottom land of Mrs. Sheppard's apple orchard. It was a great place to play. The rusty piece of machinery held great fascination. Its cab full of cobwebs, the boiler was home to mice and sparrows. At different times, it was a chariot, a spaceship to Mars, or in this case, a perfectly good stand-in for a Sherman tank. The surrounding vines and entanglements of the orchard looked exactly like the boscage countryside of France. Janie clambered down off the tractor.

"Janie, I swear you get weirder and creepier every day."

"Shut up!" Janie stuck out her tongue. Sid was a rat! That didn't make up for the apprehension she felt in the pit of her stomach. The supreme sense of dread and guilt as she walked slowly up the path to the house. When she crept to the back porch, she paused to listen. Her mother was on the phone.

". . . Yes sir, I understand, but Janie hasn't come home. I'm worried sick. We have no idea where she's gone. I'm afraid Mr. McConaughey is out of town. Sidney and John are out right now looking for her. Yes sir, as soon as she comes home. Yes, I'll call you."

"Hi, Mom," Janie said sheepishly. She didn't even try to pretend like nothing was the matter, everything was the matter. She was in big trouble. It was late, half-past-six o'clock, supper on the table was cold. She stood in front of her mother, barefoot, her school dress torn, her hair disheveled and her Dale Evans lunch box dented and battered.

"Oh, Janie!" Paula was both relieved and furious. She resisted the urge to hug her daughter. She was so angry. This was by far the worst thing Janie had ever done. "That was the Sheriff! He's on his way over right now. The Sheriff said you jumped little Bobby Segee, beat him up! The boy is in the hospital right now, seven stitches! What do you have to say for yourself, young lady?"

Janie hung her head, "I'm sorry, Mom . . ."

"Sorry doesn't help!" Paula was beside herself with anguish. "What's that on your dress? Is that blood? Oh, god, what have you done!" Paula grabbed Janie by the cheeks and squeezed. "This is serious, Janie! Look at me—you put a boy in the hospital today! The sheriff is coming for you—this time, he's going to take you to jail! A real jail, with iron bars, where you get only peas to eat and use a toilet with no seat!" Paula's clear intention was to frighten her daughter.

Janie remained stoic. "He's not so little, besides, it wasn't me . . . It was 5."

"Liar!" Paula snapped. Before she could stop herself, she slapped Janie across the face. "Goddamn you! Will you for once in your life tell me the truth! There's a little boy in the hospital, and they say you bit him!" Paula was unable to control her anger any longer. She grabbed her daughter by the arm and half-carried and half-dragged her across the kitchen floor and flung her into the closet behind the washing machine. Janie never cried.

"You stay there and think about what you did!"

Two hours passed; it was a quarter-to-eight. "Where the hell is that damn sheriff?" There was a knock on the back door. "Finally!" Paula McConaughey was at her wit's end. Frustrated, frightened, exasperated, she'd struck her own daughter, locked her in the closet, and now she had to deal with the sheriff. Except it was not the sheriff, it was the neighbor boy, Charlie Reilly.

"Mrs. McConaughey . . ." Charlie could see Janie's mother had been crying.

"Go home Charlie, this is not a good time—if you've come to see Janie, she is being punished."

"Mrs. McConaughey, please," Charlie stammered, "I didn't exactly come to see Janie—I came to see you." Charlie swallowed hard. Charlie wasn't a brave boy. His only fear in life worse than facing a live audience was his fear of confronting adults. Charlie stared into the face of a distraught Mrs. McConaughey. He wasn't sure he could do this.

"Well, Charlie, what do you want?"

"I come to tell you about Janie, about what happened."

Charlie was determined to tell the truth. Janie was his friend. He owed her that much. Once he got started, it all came spilling out like tea from a kettle. "Bobby Segee is a rat fink, a thief, and a bully! He called me a four-eyed-queer and stole thirty-two cents! He pushed Janie down. That's when they got into a scuffle, they were both on the ground, and he was going to hurt her real bad. I guess that's when she bit him. There weren't nothing else she could do Mrs. McConaughey. I swear!" Charlie was breathless.

"Did that bastard touch my daughter?"

"No ma'am, I reckon she bit him a for he got a chance."

"Does Sheriff Ficano know this?"

"No ma'am, I don't think so."

"Come into the kitchen Charlie, the Sheriff will be here in a few minutes. I want you to tell him exactly what you told me."

"Janie, I'm so sorry. I didn't know." Paula approached the closet. "Did he touch you, sweetheart?" Paula opened the door. If what she expected to find was one very small, very sorry, eleven-year-old girl, ready to go quietly upstairs to bed, she was sorely disappointed. The Janie Paula confronted was full of defiance, without the slightest hint of remorse or contrition. She was crouched over an open shoebox containing Paula's best Sunday-go-to-meet'n shoes. A dribble of spittle glistened on her daughter's chin.

"5 spit and spit, and when it gets some more spit, 5 is gonna spit again!"

Paula's sympathy evaporated in the face of this new recalcitrant behavior. She slammed the closet door, afraid of what she might do.

Sheriff Ficano took Charlie's statement and concluded his investigation. The Segee boy confessed from his hospital bed. There were no charges. It all amounted to an unfortunate after-school scuffle.

Sheriff Ficano released the clutch and the big black Chevrolet began to coast in reverse down the McConaughey driveway. He put on the brake and picked up his case notebook. Ficano paused to light a cigarette. He remained in a quandary. There was one fact about this case that he found troubling. How on earth could one very small eleven-year-old girl kick the crap out of a boy almost twice her size? It just didn't make sense.

* * *

"Fuck!" Bobby Segee fled the vacant lot behind Quigley's store, bloodied and bruised, his ego wounded worse than his body. His balls ached where the crazy bitch kicked him. Blood seeped from his cheek, he felt his face. A chunk of his cheek hung loose. The little bitch bit off half his face! He didn't dare to go home; his pap would give him worse if he ever found out he'd been bested by a girl. No, he couldn't go home.

Maybe just a little one . . . that always made him feel better. Bobby Segee dug in his pocket. The match sputtered to life. The little flame danced and flickered at the end of the wooden stick, mesmerizing him. He tossed it in a garbage bin. The little fire flickered, feebly at first, then a tongue caught a lick of grease, and the flames shot up. Bobby dashed down the back alley and turned the corner. Only then did he dare look back to admire his handy work. He watched with perverse fascination as the tiny flame he had ignited grew into a full-fledged conflagration. He was Prometheus! He watched the beast to which he'd given birth grow; it consumed the fuel in the garbage can and then erupted up the side of the tool shed, hungry for more. The fire was alive now; it leaped to the roof in a blazing, feeding, phlogiston frenzy. Bobby fantasized as his nightmares came to life. He imagined the flames as wild horses, sent by the apocalypse to trample, consume, and destroy. Only the distant wail of police sirens jerked Bobby back into reality. Bobby fled the scene. He allowed himself a fleeting glance back. There, in the midst of the purifying blaze, he could clearly see the McConaughey girl, screaming.

* * *

"School will be out in a couple of days."
"Un-huh."

"I'll be going to high school in the fall. I guess we won't be seeing each other very much after that." Charlie was feeling very melancholy.

"We can still mess around this summer." Janie tried to sound positive. "Besides, we still gotta finish the scenery for *La Travesty.*"

"Janie, don't be so goofy, it's *La Traviata!* I told you a hundred times."

"Oh, I forgot," Janie said with a coy grin.

"What you got for lunch, anyway?"

"Peanut butter, Mom always packs me peanut butter. She says it's *newtweesus* . . . how about you?"

"Tuna, I hate tuna," Charlie said.

"Wanna trade?" Janie sat beside her best friend Charlie, which was unusual enough by itself because Charlie was a boy in the eighth grade and Janie was in the fifth. This alone broke an unspoken schoolyard anathema; the older grades never fraternize with little kids. Worse yet, Janie was a girl.

Charlie didn't care, after all, why should he? What did he have to lose? It wasn't as if he had any real friends. All his classmates at Charter Oak Grammar School hated him for one reason or another. Ronnie-Ray hated him because he wasn't good at sports. Richard Vanderbilt and the smart kids hated him because Charlie wasn't good at math, science, or geography. Crissy Greene with her huge you-know-whats, and the rest of the girls hated him—well, the feeling was mutual.

Charlie and Janie sat on the bench. They sat beside each other on the farthest reaches of the playground next to the teeter-totters. The creepy girl and the quirky boy traded sandwiches. Sure, Janie was a girl, but Janie wasn't like the other girls. Janie was different. *Different,* yeah right, Charlie did his best to suppress a snicker. Janie wasn't just different, Janie was loony, off-her-trolley, bats-in-her-belfry, and certifiably mad-as-a-hatter. Did anyone ever mention that Janie was crazy? Crazy or not, Charlie didn't care. Janie didn't judge him, she accepted him for who he was. Janie was fun to be around. She laughed at his jokes, listened to him perform opera on the ukulele, and cheered his puppet shows.

Janie and Charlie couldn't have been more different, and yet they were so much alike. Janie, her head forever in the clouds, possessed with a fantastic imagination and a menagerie of people who didn't exist. Charlie, the peculiar boy who liked puppets, enamored with a desire to be a comedian. The queer boy who hated girls, whose best friend just happened to be a girl—and the girl whose head wasn't screwed on so tight. The two outcasts sat by themselves and traded sandwiches, and that made all the difference.

"Bet'cha can't guess what I got."

"What you got, tell me, please!" Janie bounced and teased, her face full of tuna fish sandwich.

"The circus is coming to town! They'll be here in Hartford next month!"

"The circus! Oh, wow, that's swell!"

"Just think of it, the Ringling Bros. and Barnum & Bailey Circus, The Greatest Show on Earth!"

Janie wasn't interested in that. She seized the colorful handbill. "Lookee here, it says see Gargantua, the world's most terrifying living creature! The Flying Wallendas and Alfred Court the lion tamer!"

"You wanna know what else? Mother sent me to Lang's drugstore to pick up a bottle of Lydia Pinkham for her *constipation* . . . Mother has terrible constipation."

Janie laughed at the way Charlie said constipation.

"I was look'n at the latest issue of *Action Comics* . . ."

"Oh, is that the one where Mr. Mxyzptlk captures Lois Lane?"

"Un-huh."

"Sid has that one, 'cept'n he won't let me read it, the rat! *'Janie, you'll only wreck it!'* " Janie put on a fake pout.

"Mr. Lang hollers to me, 'n says . . ." Charlie hunched over and made a comical, crotchety face. "Are you Charles Reilly's son?"

"Mr. Mxyzptlk, he's from the fifth dimension!" Janie interrupted, desirous to impress Charlie with her "Superman knowledge."

"I thought I was in trouble for reading ol' Mr. Lang's comics —you know how he hates it when kids read his comics without buying. Guess what, he gave me two free tickets to the circus!"

"Gee that's swell! Oh, take me, please! I want to see the lion tamers!"

"Ladies and Gentlemen!" Charlie took center ring. He looked especially dapper in his scarlet huntsman coattails and white jodhpurs and black top hat. "The Ringling Bros. and Barnum & Bailey Circus is proud to present Janie Firefly and her amazing cats!"

Merle Evans and the band struck up a lively march. The spotlights swished and circled and coalesced on the center steel cage. Janie, dressed in jungle khaki and a pith helmet, bowed to the crowd. The steel chutes opened and one, two, three fierce Siberian tigers bounded into the ring. Janie cracked her whip and signaled to Wednesday, who raised the bars on the lion chute, and three more animals took their places. Next came the black panthers. Janie was surrounded by nine great cats. Janie signaled once more, the band's music rose to a crescendo as the stark glare of the klieg spotlight centered on the empty pedestal.

The crowd gasped as bestial 5 tore out of the steel chute and took its place on the center pedestal. 5 roared—the circus spectators were spellbound as one lone girl dared to enter a steel cage surrounded by nine wild carnivores and one terrible thing. The danger was palpable. Janie cracked her whip, brandished a chair, and began to put the great cats through their paces. The mixed cats were all natural enemies. The largest of the Siberian tigers, *Tahir,* hissed and lashed out. 5 bared its yellow fangs and snarled so fiercely the crowd reacted in horror. The great Siberian cat retreated, leaving 5 the undisputed king of beasts.

"Janie!"

Janie, lost in a psychotic paroxysm, leaped to the top of the teeter-totter and roared so fiercely she made herself hoarse. Charlie was no longer afraid of 5. He knew somehow that Janie would never hurt him; instead, he concentrated on getting the silly girl down before she fell off backwards and broke her fool neck!

Janie cracked her whip. 5 was an indefatigable beast, a monster that could never be controlled. Without warning, the number turned on its mistress. The terrible id lashed out— one swipe of its mighty claw smashed the chair to kindling. Janie reeled and smacked Charlie hard upside the head with her Dale Evans lunch box. The visceral sensation of the hollow tin box contacting Charlie's skull was enough to bring an end to the psychotic episode. A portend in Janie's eye signaled she was once again in touch with reality.

"Ow, cut it out! Quit fool'n around!"

"Gee, I'm sorry," Janie said sheepishly. She'd hit her best friend with her lunch box, and she was at once very sorry. She felt foolish and ashamed and, for the first time, out-of-control. "It was just that 5 . . ." Janie started to cry.

"Shhh, forget about it."

Janie climbed down off her perch and put her head in Charlie's lap. "Chucky, what's wrong with me?"

"Noth'n, kiddo."

Janie continued to sob. Charlie held her head in his lap. He looked around, hoping nobody was watching. Charlie wanted desperately to do something; he wanted to console his friend, to comfort her in a tender, meaningful way. His cowardly hand shrank at the last second. Janie was hurting, and he was failing as her friend. Charlie felt awkward; his own neurotic inhibitions made him feel so uncomfortable that he decided he much preferred getting hit in the head with a lunch box than to have a sobbing girl in his lap.

"What I was trying to tell you—is the tickets aren't exactly free," Charlie said softly, "I got to hand out two hundred handbills. I was sorta hope'n you might want to help?"

Janie sat up and sniffed. Her face brightened, "Like we was regular advance men!" Janie's initial excitement evaporated and her expression returned to one of consternation. She bit her lip and added pensively, "Only two tickets?"

"Sure, how many tickets do we need?"

"I can't go."

"What do you mean you can't go, why not? Don't tell me it's because you're a Methodist. Your parents let you go to the movies all the time. This is the circus—it's no different than the movies, only like ten times better!"

Janie stared down at her shoes, her new black saddle shoes, bought with the precious ration coupons. The coupons Mr. Paradise gave her. "I can't go, that's all."

"It's because of me, isn't it? I knew it! Drat, crud, fud, and fudge! Every time I make a friend, something like this always happens!" Charlie got up in a huff. "Go on, Janie McConaughey, get lost! I'm glad I'm going to high school! That way, I'll never have to see you again!"

"Chucky!" Janie's voice was soft and pensive. "You are my friend, but I still can't go . . . I just can't go, not without all my friends."

Janie's revelation came as an epiphany; forced to choose between her imaginary friends and her real-life friends, Janie was caught in an impossible dilemma. For the first time, Charlie understood the height, width, and depth of Janie's psychosis. These were real people, and her loyalty to them was just as strong as her loyalty to him. Charlie made his decision.

"Hey, don't be such a chowder-head!" Charlie playfully smacked the girl upside the back of the head, payback he figured for hitting him with her dinner pail. "I got a great idea. What say when we pass out these handbills, we collect soda bottles? Mr. Lang will pay us two cents for every bottle. That way on circus day we can buy tickets for Wednesday and Holly J.!"

Janie's distraught face turned to joy. Her dimples illuminated her smile. "Oh, Chucky, that's a swell idea!"

Chapter 4

The V-Letter

Janie sat, forlorn, in intractable silence, on the hardwood floor just in front of the screen door in the foyer. Janie had troubles. She stared into space, not thinking much about anything as she waited for the postman, Mr. Griswold.

It was a nice foyer, a nice house. Janie knew she was lucky to live in such a nice house. The war continued to rage in Europe, there were millions of children, boys and girls just like her all across England, France, and Eastern Europe with dirty faces that were suffering, starving, dying even. They didn't have nice houses to live in, or enough food to eat. If they were lucky, they lived in a bombed-out hovel and ate crusts of stale bread for supper. Millions of people lived and died in constant terror of the Nazi Blitz and suffered intolerably under the heel of Hitler's jackboot thugs. Janie knew this; she went to the movies every Saturday and watched the newsreels.

Janie was miserable. She knew she had no cause to complain; she was being selfish, foolish, maybe even a little unpatriotic. America was at war. To an eleven-year-old girl, the war seemed a distant, far away, abstract idea. The United States was a rich industrial nation, defended by two great oceans. This sense of invulnerability spawned a mindset of isolationism; it was a European problem, a European war. No less a great American than Charles Lindbergh led the isolationist movement: *America First.* All that changed after Pearl Harbor. Everything changed—now this was America's war.

Despite individual sacrifices, Americans remained largely untouched by the privations of war. Sure, there were the little things, with war-time food rationing, meat was in short supply, but there were plenty of vegetables from the Victory garden. Supper was always hot and plentiful, although Janie decided secretly that when the war was over, when she grew up, she was never, ever going to eat macaroni again!

Janie's father moved the family to Hartford from Chicago and bought the house for $8,600 cash money, out of a stipend paid by the University. It was a big comfortable house, and Janie reminded herself how lucky she was to live in such a nice house. Janie had her own room; her oldest brother, John, had his own room, too. Her perfectly vulgar younger brother, Sid, and littlest Robert Jr., shared a room, which was just fine by her. There was a large living room dominated by the walnut cabinet of the RCA Victor radio, a sofa, sideboard, and a couple of overstuffed chairs. There was an airy kitchen, bright and fresh with the smells of baking, where each morning the family took breakfast. A formal dining room, Mother and Father's bedroom, and another room that was once the "servant's quarters" that Daddy recently turned into his study. One small bathroom served the whole household.

Janie was pretty sulky these days. She sat in the foyer, in front of the screen door, slashed with its diagonal wire bracing. This was her prison, her boundary. Janie couldn't go outside. She couldn't play. She couldn't listen to her favorite program: *Little Orphan Annie* on the RCA Victor. She couldn't even read from volume twelve of *The Book of Knowledge.* This was especially provoking because Janie was in the middle of reading *The Tales of the Arabian Knights.* A perfectly marvelous, wonderful story about a boy named Aladdin who found a magic lamp and when he rubbed it—a terrible djinn appeared. Oh, how she wished she had a magic lamp. *Djinn of the magic lamp, make this all go away!*

Janie was a bad girl. She was being punished. Under an arrangement agreed to by Sheriff Ficano, her mother walked her to the bus stop. Mr. Hooker, the principal, escorted her to her classroom. There was no recess; Janie ate her lunch at her desk in solitary silence while Miss Knich corrected spelling papers. She hadn't talked to Chucky for three whole days. When she came home, she did her homework, and then there was nothing—nothing to do but sit and stare through the screen door at the glorious tantalizing freedom of the whole outdoors. When the clock in the hall struck eight o'clock, just about the time the summer's fireflies made their appearance, it was time to go to bed.

"Mother is so unfair!"

"Your mother is a witch!" Holly J. said.

"Shut-up, upidstay! You've gotten me in enough trouble as it is."

"Why, what did I do? It wasn't me, blame 5 . . . if that Segee boy knew what was good for him, he never should have messed with 5! If you ask me, 5 is nothing but trouble. I don't think you should let it come around anymore."

"I can't control 5, you know that . . ." Janie sighed. Ooh, Holly J. could be so annoying sometimes, and it didn't help matters any that she was right. Janie's eyes brightened when she caught sight of Mr. Griswold, the postman, in his crisp crowned hat and distinctive blue uniform. She watched as he turned onto Stuart. He sorted and shuffled and dutifully poked a wad of letters into D-205, and methodically, deliberately proceeded up the sidewalk to Janie's house. There was a letter!

"Well?"

"Well, what?"

"Aren't you gonna get the mail?" Wednesday asked. "Could be sumpt'n important!"

"I'm not supposed to go outside."

"You still got chores, don't you?" Holly J. said, "Mother makes you take out the trash, don't she? Get'n the mail is just the same as take'n out the trash. It's a chore, ain't it?" Holly J. was such a barrister.

"I suppose."

Janie was careful not to slam the front door and alert Mother. She crept off the front porch, down the driveway to the mailbox. The sudden rush of being outside was exhilarating. The warm sunshine on her face made her forget all her troubles. For a moment, she contemplated putting on her skates. Oh, to feel the rough bump and gravel of the uneven sidewalk under her skate wheels! Just ten minutes, down to the end of the block and back. No, she'd better not, just get the mail, go back inside. Janie opened the mailbox; the hinge creaked like the door of a haunted house. Janie was certain Mother could hear.

Janie reached inside, felt around; there was just one letter. One crummy letter. It was wafer thin, on tissue paper as fragile as a gossamer wing. It was a V-letter! Janie read the address, Mrs. Robert McConaughey, then she read the return, Lieutenant Robert Clayton, 746 Battalion, Portsmouth, England. It was a letter from her Uncle Bud! Janie's heart skipped a beat.

"*Pssst*, Janie!"

Janie's heart really skipped a beat. She was caught red-handed. There she was, on the front walk, where she knew she wasn't supposed to be. She was in so much trouble.

"Janie, over here."

"Oh, jeepers! You scared me half-to-death."

"I've been waiting for you for the longest time. Where the heck have you been? You didn't come out at recess. You didn't come over after school—you didn't even call."

"I can't. Not for the rest of the year—not for the rest of my life, not forever. I'm in big trouble Chucky, on account 'cos 5 bit Bobby Segee. Sheriff Ficano says I'm *incorrihorrible*."

"Incorrigible, that's what you are," Charlie snickered.

"Yeah, that too."

"What about the circus? The circus will be in Hartford 'n two weeks. I got two-hundred hand-bills to paste. I can't do this by myself. You promised!"

"Gee, dunno, I can't. I gotta go. If Mom catches me outside, I'm in big trouble!"

"How 'bout tomorrow? Tomorrow is Saturday—they can't keep you locked up forever."

They just might. Janie thought about the djinn of the magic lamp and her three wishes. She wished she could go with Chucky tomorrow. It wasn't as if it was all her fault, it was 5—it was mostly stupid Bobby Segee's fault. Janie's feisty rebel spirit welled up, nobody was going to tell her what to do. Not Mother, not Mr. Hooker, least of all not that fat wop goombah Sheriff Ficano!

"We gotta have a plan," Janie said. "You come over tomorrow, ten o'clock, come to my window . . . Mother does laundry on Saturday. She'll be busy all day. Keep it quiet. Real sneaky, like we was spies!" Janie flashed a sly dimpled grin, "See you later, crocodile."

"Shut up, Daffy Duck."

* * *

Janie slammed the screen door, extra loud, in a rebellious act of deliberate defiance. She knew there was nothing mother could do. She held in her hand the V-letter, which trumped all of Mother's stupid rules.

"Mom! We got a V-letter, it's from Uncle Bud!" Janie burst into the kitchen and tracked clear across Paula's freshly waxed floor. For once, it didn't matter. Paula dropped the bottle of Johnson Glo-Coat, a V-letter! She clutched the letter to her breast. Her brother was alive! Ever since that terrible day, the sixth of June, Paula became a ghost. She tried to keep up a brave face, washing, ironing; the children were fed, off to school on time. Inside, she was dying.

Every night, the family gathered around the radio and listened to the reports of the D-Day invasion. The brave soldiers of the combined Allied expeditionary force were making steady progress, yet at what price? The papers were full of reports of the horrific slaughter on the Normandy beaches. Places with innocuous-sounding names like *Omaha, Sword, and Juno.* Paula's heart was choked with fear as she imagined the fate of her brother's unit. Paula's brother was a tanker, in command of a Sherman tank. The tanks were expected to swim ashore in the rough chop of the English Channel. Thirty-three tons of dead weight, with German bullets whizzing all around, and only a flimsy canvas screen to keep them afloat. They seemed so utterly fragile, foolish, and funny, Hobart's funnies they called them.

Last Christmas, Bud came home on furlough. He was pretty cavalier about the whole expected invasion. The Allies were assembled, two million American, British and Canadian soldiers, thousands of ships, airplanes, and landing craft, the greatest invasion force in history, poised to invade Hitler's fortress Europe. The whole invasion was a little like hiding an elephant under a rug. Everybody knew it was coming; indeed, the Allies expended a great deal of effort convincing everyone (including the Germans), that the invasion embarkation point was the *Pas de Calais.* This was deliberate subterfuge. When the Normandy invasion came, it was a shock to everyone.

Paula said she was afraid. Bud just laughed. Bud was a big joker. He lifted Janie on his knee and pretended to teach his niece how to double-clutch a Sherman gearbox. *Varoom!* What could be better? French girls, French wine, *Ooh, la, la . . .* driving around the French countryside in a Sherman tank, with two-inches of steel armor between him and the Jerrys.

"Don't worry, Paula. We'll be in Paris by September. It's a cakewalk!"

Paula wasn't so sure. She listened to the radio; she read the bold black face headlines in the *Hartford Courant.* Her husband Robert sat every night, with his map and magnifying glass, charting faraway places with strange-sounding names like *Tobruk, Bizerte, El Alamein*—in North Africa, where the Germans inflicted horrific losses on British tankers. The Germans had a terrible kind of gun, an eighty-eight, they called it—that could open up a Sherman like a tin of sardines. Paula was afraid; her hands trembled as she tore open the thin paper seal.

"Don't worry, Mom, Uncle Bud, he's okay. He's in the hospital, a German shell fragment." Janie's words were entirely innocent, yet doomed with an otherworldly prophecy.

June 13, 1944

Dearest Paula,

Me 'n the boys landed in rough chop. The surf drove us half a mile off our landing zone. The beaches are treacherous, and the Krauts are everywhere. They shot at us, but their bullets bounced off our armor. We took out a pillbox.

I haven't had a bath or a hot meal in ten days! I brag to the boys about your good home cook'n! I sure wish I could have one of your potpies right now! Heck, I'd settle for a decent cup of coffee!

We stopped the tank just long enough for the engineers to take off our canvas "swimming skirts." Then the welders got busy and fitted us with something called a "rhino." We are in the hedgerow country of Brittany now. There are Germans everywhere! Remember when we used to play in Mr. Raymond's backyard and how proud he was of his hedges? Well, I have to tell you I've never seen hedges so tall in all my life! Sixteen feet! Thank God the engineers fitted us with those rhinos. We go busting through those hedges like gang-busters!

Now for the bad news, please don't worry Paula. I'm fine, just a scratch. A piece of jerry shrapnel caught me in the shoulder. I should be out of the hospital and rejoin my unit in two weeks.
Kiss Janie for me.
Love,
Bud

Paula looked up. She was visibly shaken. "Janie, how did you know your Uncle Bud was wounded?" Paula sank to her knees, teetering somewhere on the precipice between furious and incredulous. She shook her daughter. "Tell me the truth, quick, none of your foolish lies. You opened this!"

"Jeepers, Mom, we was just playing, that's all . . . Uncle Bud got hit, that's what happened."

Paula looked into her daughter's face as if she possessed some other-worldly powers. This time, there was only honesty, no deception. But with Janie, you could never be sure what was real and what was fantasy. Was she touched? Did she have a gift? Paula did not know.

* * *

Saturday morning came, bright and full of promise; it was the last Saturday weekend before school let out for summer. There were just two more days of school, Monday and Tuesday, and Tuesday was a half-day, and as such, hardly counted. Every boy and girl all across Connecticut waited with palpable anticipation for the beginning of summer vacation. The boys and girls of Hartford were especially excited because in three short weeks, not only was there the usual promise of parades, hot dogs, and fireworks on the fourth of July, but the next day the circus was coming to town.

Not Janie. Janie came down for breakfast with her bathrobe blowsy, and her pajama top buttoned two-buttons wrong. Her hair disheveled, her face contorted into a confirmed funk. Janie was in a no-good mood, a rotten mood. Janie was being punished; she couldn't go out and play, she couldn't listen to the radio, she couldn't read from *The Book of Knowledge*. She couldn't do nothing. She scowled at her brother, Sid, as if her misfortunes were somehow all his fault. Sid retorted, with in-your-face *schadenfreude*.

"Mom, I think I'll go play catch in the park . . . and then maybe I'll go down to Hog Creek to catch tadpoles."

"Be back by lunchtime, darling."

Janie scoffed, (Sid was a rat, her brother knew how much she liked catching tadpoles)! Janie ate her breakfast of oatmeal, toast, and orange juice in monastery silence. After breakfast, she helped Mother wash and dry the dishes.

Janie returned to her room to sulk. Well, not really. Janie's world was far too engrossing for her to sulk for very long. Janie stole some of Sid's green army men and set up a line of soldiers. She arranged the tan soldiers on the other side. They were the Japs. Then she took his toy P-38 Lightning and practiced strafing runs on the Jap soldiers.

Janie's imagination soared. She dreamed of being a fighter ace in the cockpit of her trusty P-38 Lightning, somewhere over Tarawa, dive-bombing, strafing the Japanese. A Jap Zeke appeared out of nowhere, automatic cannons blazing. She was ambushed on her six o'clock. The plane was hit. Her canopy shot away, engines on fire! The Rolls-Royce Merlins smoked and sputtered, the port engine conked out for good. She was going down! The jungle swirled beneath her.

The air-raid siren . . .

The long, lonely wail of the air-raid siren broke the stillness of the Saturday morning. It started with a low moan and built to a crescendo, then faded and started again. The sound was one of absolute fear.

Every Saturday morning at precisely ten o'clock, the city of Hartford held an air-raid drill. Every citizen knew what he was supposed to do. Everyone was to take cover, head for the nearest air-raid shelter. Every boy and girl knew what to do— this was taught in school, every boy and girl, that is, except for Janie. Oh, Janie knew what to do all right, it was just that Janie wasn't particularly thinking about air-raid drills or civil defense. She was far too preoccupied thinking about Japanese Zeros. . . . Her Lockheed P-38 Lightning locked in a deadly embrace of aerial combat somewhere over Tarawa. Janie pulled back on the stick, punched the Coffman starter and the big Rolls-Royce coughed, shuttered, then roared to life. The jungle canopy filled her view.

"Pull up, pull up!"

Careless, arrogant, confident of victory, the Japanese Zeke circled overhead, its underbelly exposed and vulnerable. Janie was pressed back into her seat to the point of blackout as the combined horsepower of the two Rolls-Royce Merlin engines clawed at the thick jungle air. The Zeke was in her cross-hairs. She pulled the trigger. The Japanese Zero exploded, disintegrated under the combined onslaught of six fifty-caliber machine guns.

The air-raid siren . . .

"Oh, crud!" The Japs are attacking! Janie remembered her plan. It was a good plan, a gosh darn clever plan.

Charlie Reilly stood in front of the McConaughey house and waited for Janie. He was oblivious to the notion that the clock was one tick away from ten o'clock. That Saturday was "air-raid drill day." Not that he didn't know; on an intellectual level, of course he knew. It was just that this was a special day;

today was the day he and Janie were going to distribute posters around town, handbills for the upcoming circus. The Ringling Bros. and Barnum & Bailey Circus, The Greatest Show on Earth, was coming to town, and it was his job to paste posters all around town. The posters, a pot of glue, and two brushes were neatly arranged in his wagon. There was a thermos, and a paper sack with two tuna fish sandwiches, that was lunch. Charlie took his job very seriously. Mr. Lang was depending on him, as was Mr. Healy, the superintendent of the circus. Charlie felt a certain amount of pride; after all, he was a show-business man himself.

Charlie imagined that in some small way, even John Ringling North was depending on him.

The siren wailed.

"Oh, crud!"

Charlie looked to Janie's window. Janie appeared, staggered, and clutched her chest. Her face was contorted. She was spattered with blood! Charlie was horrified.

Never bold, brash, or bumptious, normally mild-mannered Charlie was not a decisive boy. This time was different. He didn't knock. He didn't ask if he might, Charlie didn't hesitate. He burst through the screen door of the McConaughey house uninvited and bounded up the stairs to Janie's room. His friend Janie was in trouble!

Thump, wump, before Charlie could react, Janie tackled him. He felt something wet and gross pour over his head.

"Get off of me! Girl, are you crazy? Lemme go!"

"Don't worry, Chucky. The Japs will never find us here! And if they do . . ." Janie splotted more ketchup on Charlie's head for good measure. "This way, they'll think we're dead!"

Charlie and Janie sat in a heap on the floor, covered in ketchup.

"Janie, you are so upidstay!"

* * *

"Hold still, you've still got ketchup in your hair!" Charlie pushed Janie's head under the bathtub faucet and washed and scrubbed as what seemed like gallons of red ketchup swirled, pooled, and ultimately washed down the drain. The bathroom was a disaster, the aftermath of Janie's brilliant master plan. The floor sloshed and squished with water splashed from the tub. The bathroom was a soggy mess of wet towels; everything stained a vaguely disconcerting, ketchupy red.

"Cut it out, Chucky—yer drown'n me. I'll take a bath later." Janie wrestled free from under the faucet and shook her head like a dog. Her short blonde hair was all spiky and tinged, and she smelt faintly of tomatoes and vinegar.

What a disaster! Charlie worried about what Mrs. Mc-Conaughey would say. Janie didn't care. Janie never seemed to care about anything based in reality. Without warning, without the slightest hint of shame or self-consciousness—Janie whipped off her wet undershirt and tossed it carelessly, casually on the floor. Charlie averted his eyes. Janie acted as if it were the most natural thing in the world. She shot Charlie a backward glance before she dashed off to her bedroom to fetch a clean camisole and a fresh summer blouse.

Aooogah, it was the klaxon horn of Mr. Paradise's Model A pickup. "Mr. Paradise, I knew he'd come!" Janie launched herself over the banister and clattered down the stairs, sounding less like an eleven-year-old girl and more like a new-shod-mule.

"Com'on, Chucky, hurry up!"

"What's going on?"

"It's Mr. Paradise, he's come to take us downtown. It'll be lots faster than that dumb ol' wagon."

Charlie grimaced; this turn of events was unplanned as it was unexpected. He'd entertained happy thoughts of spending a special day with Janie. Now everything was spoiled.

His thirteen-year lifelong struggle of accumulated insecurities, inhibitions, and neuroses suddenly came to this paroxysm. Charlie felt something twist in the pit of his stomach. It wasn't exactly anger; he was sure he wasn't feeling sick. Charlie was certain he'd never felt quite this way before. Janie was Charlie's best friend, and for the first time in his life, Charlie felt jealous —the worst part of it was—the most confusing part was— he felt jealous over a girl!

* * *

"Hallo, Tochter!"

Janie ran and jumped on the running board of the big black Ford Truck. "Mr. Paradise!"

"Well, if it isn't my good friend Janie Firefly. Telling me,

fräulein, Frau Detweiler said that you telephoned, something important, no?"

"Mr. Paradise, can you give us a ride around town?" For the first time, Janie noticed the big green "B" gas rationing sticker in the back window, not the usual "A" sticker issued to all non-essential drivers that limited everyday ordinary people to just four gallons of gasoline a week. Her friend, Mr. Paradise, was somebody important!

"Your mother, father,they are okay with this?" Jim remained cautious.

"Oh, sure," Janie lied. Mother was in the backyard, hanging up the laundry. There was a fresh breeze that morning. Janie imagined the snap and crack of the billowing sheets. Mother would be busy for hours!

"Telling me fräulein, who is your young friend here?"

"Oh, that's just Chucky—we're gonna be advance men for the circus!"

Jim got out of his truck and walked around to the other side. "Pleased to making your acquaintance, Herr Chucky." Jim extended his hand.

Charlie shook hands reluctantly with the stranger and continued to assess the threat presented by this obtruder. It was clear from the way she acted, Janie was most powerfully preoccupied, infatuated with this old man. She worshiped the ground he walked on. How could he compete? Inadequate didn't even begin to describe the way Charlie felt; he was bush-league, inept, and small potatoes. Janie was smitten, enthralled with a grown-up who drove a truck with a "B" sticker. How could he compete with that?

"It's Charlie, sir, and we're only going as far as downtown."

"That's good because that's as far as I can take you. I have work to be doing, young Herr Charlie." Mr. Paradise helped load the wagon, and two friends and the old man drove off.

From behind the secretive confines of the living room blinds, Sidney watched his sister and waited. Sidney was per-fectly willing to watch the whole scene unfold. He never said nothing; instead, he relished the moment, waiting for the opti-mum time to pounce. Janie had run away, absconded, with the creepy neighbor boy who played with dolls and a strange old man in a truck.

"Oh, Boy! This was too good to be true!"

This unexpected act of supreme disobedience was so de-liciously profound as not to be squandered. Sidney considered his options. If he played his cards right, he might have the pleasure of listening to his sister get her ass whupped, her mouth washed out with soap, and shut in the closet behind the washing machine. Sid cackled with glee. That would fix her big swinging butt for good! The time came to cash in on his colossal tattle-tale coup. Sidney calculated his words for maximum parental panic.

"Mom! Janie drove off with a strange man in a truck!"

* * *

Janie and Charlie walked up one side of the street and down the other. The two friends had been walking for hours. They sat on the curb in a general disposition of despair. Janie had glue in her hair; the back of her neck was sunburned. Charlie took off his shoes and rubbed his sore feet. It was three o'clock, and the children were exhausted. The tuna fish sandwiches and thermos of milk were long since forgotten. They had walked what seemed like five hundred miles and pasted almost one hundred posters and collected twenty-four bottles, for which Mr. Lang would pay forty-eight cents. Grandstand tickets cost $1.25. They were still two dollars and two cents short. It seemed like a lot of walking for an awful lot of nothing.

"It's your turn to pull the wagon."

Janie put on a pout.

"Cheer up, kiddo," Charlie said, trying to remain optimistic. "We still have two more weeks. We can collect lots more bottles by then."

"It won't make any difference," Janie said in a small voice. "I think you'd better take me home. I want to go home—I can't go with you to the circus, no matter how many soda bottles we collect. Not now, not ever! There's sumpt'n I didn't tell you . . . Mother doesn't know I took off—I'm not supposed to leave the house."

"Cripes, Janie! Why-the-heck did you have to go and do that? Your mother is gonna blow her top!" Charlie couldn't believe this was happening. With the help of that old kraut, he once again found himself ensnared in one of Janie's acts of chicanery. The consequence of this latest bit of less-than-trifling subterfuge: he found himself caught, criminally culpable in the kidnapping of his best friend! He was in big trouble! Charlie's panicked brain conjured up all manners of sensational headlines in the *Hartford Courant:*

HARTFORD GIRL MISSING
Eleven-year-old girl Janie McConaughey kidnapped!
Eighth-Grader Charles Reilly suspected in kidnapping plot.

Janie didn't seem all that terribly cut-up about the pending consequences, as to her running away, or about anything else that amounted to any real seriousness. She sat down on the curb alongside Charlie and fretted. What was really on her mind, what was really bothering her, was that they had not collected enough soda bottles to pay for Holly J. and Wednesday to go to the circus.

"What are we gonna do, Chucky?"

"About you running away? About me kidnapping you?"

"No, goosey, about the soda bottles!" Charlie thought for a moment, he paused; maybe, there was something he could do. Charlie took off his glasses and nervously twisted them between his thumb and forefinger. Well, it just might work . . . Maybe he could swap one dummy for another dummy. "Gimme your handkerchief."

"Why, what for?" Janie was reluctant. It was a pretty floral design, one Grams had given her, an especially girly handkerchief. Charlie didn't seem to mind. He flipped and snapped the handkerchief and tied it around his neck in a jaunty bow.

"Gotta have a costume."

Charlie reached underneath the wagon wheel and retrieved a lick of axle grease.

"Ew! Whatcha gonna do with that?"

"Hold still." Charlie drew two vertical lines, one on either side of Janie's chin, and blackened her eyebrows. "Now come'er, and sit on my lap. I want you to act like you're a puppet made of wood. When I tap on you, I want you to move your mouth, but don't say a word. I'll do all the rest."

Janie crinkled her nose. "Chucky, this is upidstay."

"Shhh, trust me, this will work."

For the first time, Charlie felt filled with self-assurance. Making jokes was what he was good at. The clumsy, gawky Charlie disappeared, and in its place was a clever, cocky comic. There on the curb, in front of G. Fox's department store, Charlie positioned Janie on his knee. He was in his element. Before even a word was spoken, a collection of curious passersby paused to watch. Charlie Reilly had them right where he wanted them. There on the street curb, with Janie on his lap, he assumed center stage.

"There's trouble at the mill!" Charlie threw his voice. His ventriloquism was nearly perfect. Janie turned her head mechanically and blinked a wooden stare. She looked comically at the audience.

"Why, what happened?" Charlie said.

"A woman fell into a lens grinder."

"That's terrible, was she killed?"

"Nah, but she made a spectacle out of herself!" The audience laughed. Janie laughed, too; she couldn't help it. Chucky was so funny!

"You're not supposed to laugh, upidstay! You're a dummy, remember?" Charlie hissed under his breath. The act continued.

"There's trouble at the mill!"

"Oh, no, not again!"

"A woman fell into a lens grinder . . . dis-ASS-ter!"

The audience laughed uproariously. Janie Firefly was a funny girl. She was crass, brash, and rude, and as Charlie's phony dummy, she was the perfect foil. She could say things that ordinarily mild-mannered, introverted Charlie could never say. Janie was a natural, sitting on his lap; she became Charlie's secret alter ego. Charlie's impeccable comedic timing sensed the time was right.

"Hey, Charlie, I hear your girlfriend, Janie, was in the beauty shop yesterday for two hours." Janie gasped when she heard the puppet speak her name. Charlie never made fun of her or made her the butt of any of his jokes. More surprising even than that was hearing Charlie refer to her as his "girlfriend." *Was she really Charlie's girlfriend?* Her heart fluttered. She almost missed her cue.

"That was just for the estimate!" Janie the puppet quirked and blinked, "She got a mudpack and looked great for two days. Then the mud fell off!"

By this time, there were almost fifty people thronged in a circle around Charlie and his live girl-dummy. Enterprising Charlie had the foresight to take off his cap. Four dollars filled his hat.

"Do you come from a big family?" Janie mimed.

"I'm an only child, but I have lots of relatives?"

"Relative to what?"

"No, like aunts 'n uncles. Take, for example, my dear Aunt Zetti on my father's side."

"Is she the one with the bad back?" Janie made a silly face.

"Yeah, she's gett'n married to a man named Henry. It's quite the family scandal. They say," Charlie whispered into Janie's ear, (loudly). "That Mr. Henry can't do it."

"Do what?" Janie's ignorance was innocent. The throng of people laughed at the dummy's innuendo.

"You know . . . do it."

"Ohhh, well, I wouldn't worry too much about that."

"Why, what do you mean?"

"It's a good match, as long as Aunt Zetti's back doesn't peter out—and Mr. Henry's peter doesn't back out!" Janie guffawed, made a quirky face, and exercised her greasepaint eyebrows. Janie was a natural. The crowd laughed uproariously at the boy and his silly girl-puppet. Charlie figured he was on to something; Janie was even funnier than his real dummy.

The act was going great—that is, until Sheriff Ficano arrived in his police cruiser and put the kibosh on the impromptu curbside performance. A single *Arrrooh* from his police siren parted the crowd.

Sheriff Ficano leaned out of his police cruiser, chomping a cigar. He was mad, pissed off, more likely. He was clearly not amused by Charlie or his bit of spontaneous street theater. Ficano extricated his bulk from his squad car.

"This girl is a runaway!" A thirty-year veteran of the force, Ficano prided himself on his cool, professional demeanor. Not this time. This girl had caused him a great deal of trouble. The child was a nuisance, a juvenile delinquent, and a trouble-maker.

"You're coming with me." There was an unmistakable measure of roughness, perhaps even a hint of malice, in the way Ficano cinched the handcuffs and wrestled one very small, frightened Janie Firefly into the back of his police cruiser.

"Chucky, I love you!" Janie blurted before Ficano ducked her head and slammed the car door shut.

Charlie never said nothing.

78 ~ S. MICHAEL MCALLISTER

Chapter 5

The Girl in the Striped Pajamas

"Mister, where are you taking me?"

"To the County Juvenile hall."

The Sheriff's voice was harsh and desolate, devoid of the slightest hint of pity or compassion. Juvenile hall. The stark words fell on Janie's ears with all the finality of a guillotine blade. She knew only very naughty, wicked children went to Juvenile hall. *Oh, you're in big trouble now, Janie McConaughey!* Janie decided this was absolutely, positively the worst thing that ever happened to her in her whole life, ever! Worse even than the dreaded check mark ◇ on the blackboard.

Janie sat fretfully in the back seat of the big black Chevrolet. The upholstery was scarred with cigarette burns; it was lumpy and smelled funny. Janie sniffed and sobbed and fought hard to hold back a floodgate of tears. For the first time, she was frightened.

"You're not gonna cry, are you?" 5 sneered and gnashed its yellow teeth. "Aw, looksee, go ahead 'n cry, show 'em what a wittle cry baby you really are!" Wicked 5 almost seemed to relish Janie's miserable plight. No, she wasn't going to cry. 5 was starting to make her mad.

"Settle down back there. Who in the blue blazes are you talking to?" Ficano shot a backward glance.

"Benedict Arnold." Holly J. couldn't resist being a smart-ass. Wednesday laughed, too, one of those suppressed "church" laughs that sort of sniggered, snorted, and snuffled out of one side of her nose. Janie, her face still red from not-exactly-crying, cracked a grin. All three girls started to laugh. The joke was on 5. They all knew 5 was too feral, too deranged to know who Benedict Arnold was.

"Mister, are you gonna blow the siren? 'Cos if you are, can I blow the siren? I've always wanted to blow the siren on a real police car."

Sheriff Ficano groaned. His cigar quivered, a huge chunk of ash fell hot in his lap. He already knew the kid was precocious, but she was turning out to be a regular pain-in-the-ass. He had no idea. Janie slipped her skinny wrist free of the handcuffs and flipped the lock on the backseat door. At forty miles an hour, around a sharp curve, the car door swung open.

"Run, Seven, Run!"

Ficano uttered an oath and slammed on the brakes. His face turned several shades of livid purple. He had visions of his suspect, the child, tumbling out of the back of his police car. To his temporary relief, a triumphant Janie was still seated in the backseat, grinning.

"He got away!"

Ficano cursed himself; it was his own fault. In his haste, he'd neglected to secure the backseat passenger-proof lock, and carelessly fastened the girl's restraints in front. This was no ordinary eleven-year-old girl. The child was a devil! The remedy was to cinch the steel manacles tight behind the girl's back like a real criminal. "Let's see you get out of that!"

The handcuffs pinched.

"Mister . . . does this mean I haf'ta pee in a toilet with no seat?"

"Shut up, kid!"

Janie was booked, fingerprinted, and thrown into a holding cell.

"We took this off her." Ficano flicked a Ronson cigarette lighter.

"That belongs to my brother-in-law." A grim-faced Robert McConaughey came straight from the train station. "Janie must have taken it from my dresser."

"Yeah, well, as you may already know, we had a suspicious fire last week, arson. Started in a trash bin, burnt down a garage, and damn near burnt down Quigley's Hardware—if the fire department hadn't arrived in time."

"You're not implying my daughter had anything to do with that."

"What I'm saying Mr. McConaughey, is . . ." Ficano slapped down a thick sheath of paper. "We are continuing to investigate all suspects. This came in from Chicago. It's a police report about another suspicious fire. A Mr. George Raymond's shed; does that jar your memory? It seems this isn't the first time your daughter's been caught playing with fire."

"This is bullshit! That fire was undetermined! Janie had nothing to do with that. I'm leaving, and I'm taking my daughter with me!"

"That girl is dangerous!" Ficano snapped, "She attacked and bit a little boy! She may have gotten off on that one, Mr. Mc-Conaughey, but this time around, I assure you I have her cold. I have witnesses who place her in the vicinity of Quigley's store. I have opportunity, motive. I have the lighter. That girl isn't going anywhere. I have more than enough evidence to hold your daughter for forty-eight hours."

"You wouldn't dare!" Robert was furious. "I'm warning you, Constable. I'll have your badge for this! Secretary Hull is a personal friend of mine."

"You don't scare me, professor, you and your Washington hot-shot intellectuals. We'll just see what Judge Borso has to say about this in the morning."

Robert stormed out. He marched straight to a phone booth, dug in his pocket for a dime, and dialed. "Hello, Operator. I need to place a long-distance person-to-person call to Washington."

For the next two hours, a flurry of phone calls and teletypes flashed between Washington, New Haven, and Hartford. With the D-Day invasion of Hitler's Fortress Europe in its seventeenth day, with the fate of Britain, France, and two million Allied soldiers hanging in the balance—suddenly it seemed the power-brokers, the politicians, the Secretary of War, and the office of Army Chief-of-Staff George C. Marshall stopped in their tracks, paused, and for a brief moment, the entire resources of the United States government were focused on the plight of one very small, naughty little girl.

"Well, you've gone and done it now," Wednesday said.

"Yeah, it's off to the big house for you kid—the clink, the pokey—its striped pajamas 'n a ball'n chain fer you, kiddo!" Holly J. was forever helpful.

"They don't lock up little kids."

"Wanna make a bet?"

Janie Firefly, convicted anarchist and enemy of the people, lay on her bunk, smoking a cigarette. Oh, sure, she'd been sent to the principal's office hundreds of times, but jail was something altogether different. She'd never been arrested before. Clad in zebra-striped pajamas, she lay, forlorn, on a bare wooden plank suspended from the wall by chains. The relentless tick of the clock, her only companion. The iron bars and oppressive gray cinderblock walls pressed in on her, suffocating her. Two hours passed, two hours since her last meal . . . her very last meal. Two hours closer to her date with ol' Sparky.

The Governor's phone did not ring, there was to be no reprieve. The hollow echo of footsteps down the hall signaled the guards were coming. A key jangled in the lock. The cell door swung open. Janie held up her hand, blinded by the light. Somewhere beyond her view, a priest recited the twenty-third Psalm. It was time.

The Mayor's office was the first to receive the call. It seemed Robert McConaughey did indeed have some very powerful friends in Washington who were not above meddling in what was otherwise a local affair. Ficano scowled, but there was nothing he could do. The order came straight from the Governor's mansion.

"Come, Janie, you're going home."

Janie's heart sank. It was not the Warden, not the Governor, it was her father. She'd almost rather have gone to the electric chair than face her father. A severe Robert McConaughey marched out of Juvenile hall with one less-than-contrite Janie Firefly in tow, her face still smudged with axle grease.

5 screeched and spat. It cursed its foul luck—claw poised, ready at the charged 5000-volt switch.

* * *

Sidney was practicing the piano. As a molehill is to a mountain, the "practicing" part was largely open to interpretation. Oh, Sid was indeed seated at a piano, and he was "playing" the piano, but only in the loosest sense of the word. Paula hovered, praised, and encouraged his every discordant miss-key with delusive applause.

♫ *C-D-E, C-D-E* ♫

"Very good, Sidney, back straight, fingers arched!"

Sidney's obsequious behavior was enough to make Janie want to vomit. She knew first-hand how much her brother hated practicing the piano. He was such a sycophant! Whereas Sidney was the constant recipient of lavish, puerile praise, Janie was the black sheep. Stricken from every book and tablet, she who shall remain nameless, banished to her bedroom . . . for all time. Her supper of cold spam, cheese, and peas lay untouched on the dresser. Mother knew how much she hated peas!

There was never any doubt that Robert McConaughey was smart, a brilliant mathematician, a statistician, with an MBA in physics and a Ph.D. in theoretical analysis. Robert was personally selected by President Roosevelt to lead a team of New Haven scientists in the development of what was to become the United States' second most secret weapon against the Nazis. The radar-controlled proximity blast artillery shell represented a quantum leap in military technology.

Ohms, G-force analysis, inscrutable artillery computation tables, these were second nature to Robert's world. The conundrum now confronting him was a hammer, a nail, and an ordinary second-floor sash window. The goal: to keep one very small, naughty eleven-year-old girl from running away. Common carpentry, it seemed, utterly befuddled him.

♫ C-D-E, C-D-E ♫

WHAM!

"Confound it!" Robert was no carpenter. He fumbled, tried to use the claw "thingy" to extract the bent nail. When that failed, as a scientist, Robert remained unperturbed. He resolved that particular experiment yielded insufficient data to draw a conclusion. His solution was to embark upon an entirely new set of experiments. He chose a new nail.

♫ C-D-E, C-D-E ♫

WHAM!

More miss-chords, more incessant hammering, all kept in peculiar syncopated time. Janie buried her head under her pillow in a failed attempt to blot out both her father's hammering and the torturous off-key chords emanating from the living room.

"There, that should do it." Robert stood back and admired his handiwork. The window casement was a mess of bent nails and donkey tracks. "There will be no more running away, young lady . . . Janie!"

"Yes Daddy, I promise, no more running away." A muffled Janie peeked out from underneath her pillows. Somewhere downstairs, Sid continued to practice his wretched piano. Her father left the room. She heard the key turn in the lock. "Oh, double crud!" Janie Firefly, convicted anarchist, insurrectionist, and political prisoner, locked away in the *Château d'If* like the Count of Monte Crisco.

No more running away, well, not very far, at least.

Janie closed her eyes; all her troubles seemed to coalesce like pigeons come home to roost. Her mind spun out of control. She wanted desperately to get away, to run away, to another place, a far-away place. Across the tempest-tossed Atlantic to the rim of North Africa, French Morocco, 1941, *Casablanket,* Charlie's Café Americain.

"Attention all playground monitors," Mr. Hooker, the Principal of Charter Oak Grammar school, his voice crackled over the PA. "Two eighth-graders were beaten up by the merry-go-round at lunchtime. Their lunches eaten and their hall passes stolen! The possible perpetrator is a fourth-grade girl headed for Casablanket. Round up all suspicious students and search them for sandwich crumbs!"

In Café Americain, Charlie sat at the bingo table, watching his ice cream sundae slowly melt. He paused to sign a credit extension for fifty cents. It was a private room. No one was allowed access without an affirmative nod from Charlie. The maître d' stopped a particularly obnoxious eighth-grader. "Monsieur, is a private room, your money is good at the soda fountain."

"This is an outrage!"

In the confusion, slithery, sleazy 5, dressed in an impeccable white evening jacket and smoking a cigarette, weaseled its way past the Maître d'. 5 strode boldly over to Charlie's table as if it were invited and pulled up a chair.

"Hello, Charlie."

5 paused; this was Charlie's place, after all, a certain amount of deference was due. "5 will sit?"

Charlie ignored 5 for the thing that it was.

"Too bad about those eighth-graders, wasn't it?"

"Yeah, too bad . . . too bad for whoever beat 'em up because when Mr. Hooker finds out, and he will find out, they'll be writing sentences on the blackboard for a week!"

"You are a very cynical person, Charlie, if you will forgive 5 for saying so."

"There's nothing to forgive."

The number grimaced and leaned closer. "You despise 5, don't you?"

"If I gave it a second thought, I probably would."

"But why? Do you object to the business 5 does?"

"That kind of business is nothing but trouble."

"Well, Charlie, after tonight it intends to settle all business." The thing scowled, its gaping jaws contorted in a jagged grimace. "5 is leaving Casablanket, look Charlie." The number reached into its breast pocket and produced two slips of yellow paper. "Do you know what these are?"

Charlie shook his head.

"Something even you have never seen. Hall passes, signed by Mr. Hooker. They cannot be rescinded or even questioned. Tonight, 5 plans to sell these hall passes for a whole dollar. Then it's good-bye, Casablanket!"

Charlie looked down at his ice-cream sundae; the cherry slid off the peak, he signaled the waiter, "Grape Nehi."

"5 has many friends in Casablanket, but somehow, since you despise 5 . . . you, Charlie, are the only one it trusts. Will you keep these safe?"

Charlie didn't like it. "For how long?"

"—An hour, perhaps a little longer."

"I won't keep them after school."

"Don't be afraid of that! Please keep them. 5 knew it could trust you." The number got up and lit a cigarette. "Waiter, 5 is expecting some people. If anybody asks, it will be right here."

The waiter brought a frosty bottle of grape Nehi on a silver tray. The id scowled, knocked the glass from the tray, tore the crown cap off with its teeth, and drank straight from the bottle. The thing exhaled deeply, "Charlie, I hope you are now more impressed with 5. If you don't mind, 5 thinks it will share its good luck at bingo."

"Not so fast, I heard rumors those two eighth-graders had hall passes."

5's yellow-green eyes narrowed to evil slits. "It heard those rumors, too."

"You're right," Charlie brushed errant crumbs of ham 'n cheese from the thing's dinner jacket. "I am a little bit more impressed."

Charlie strolled casually out onto the café floor, past a clan-destine game of high-stakes jacks, and where the fourth-grade boys were shooting marbles. Sid, the piano player, was prac-ticing his scales. Charlie sauntered over to the piano player and surreptitiously secreted the forbidden hall passes in the piano box.

Janie Firefly stepped out of the taxi; this was her first time in Casablanket. She wore a stylish white dress and carried a clutch purse. Janie stood in front of Charlie's Café Americain. It had been a long time. The maître d' instantly recognized her and ushered her to a private table. "Orange Nehi for made-moiselle."

"Merci." Janie sipped her drink, "Oh, waiter, could you have the piano player come over here."

"Oui, mademoiselle."

Sid eased his piano across the café floor and sat down on the stool. "Hello, Sid."

"Hello, Sis. It's been a long time."

"Yeah, like since breakfast. Did you pass your spelling test?"

"Yes, Sis, a lot of water under the bridge since then." Sid fumbled with his sheet music.

"Some of the old songs . . ."

"Sure thing, Sis."

"Where's Chucky?"

"I don't know. I ain't seen him all night."

"When will he be back?"

"Not tonight, he went home."

"Does he always leave so early?"

"I'm not supposed to say, but sometimes he meets a girl, Crissy Greene, over at the Lincoln Dairy."

Janie snickered, how absurd. The thought of Chucky with another girl—Chucky hated girls! "You used to be a much better liar." Janie paused to take a sip of her orange soda.

"Leave him alone, you're noth'n but bad luck to him."

"Play it once, Sid, for old time's sake." Janie smiled; her dimples rivaled the sparkle of her diamond broach.

"I don't know what you mean."

"Play it, Sid."

"I can't remember it, I'm a little rusty."

"I'll hum it for you . . . *dah, de, de dah de dum.*"

Sid shook his head. "Boss won't like it." Sid acquiesced and reluctantly began the first few tentative chords. As the evocative notes charged the air, Charlie stormed out of his office, furious the piano player had disobeyed his orders never to perform that song. Charlie is caught short, shocked to see Janie

Firefly sitting, radiant, her eyes brimming glassy with tears and bittersweet memories' past.

If the situation were not awkward enough, Captain Wednesday, the local préfet, chose that exact moment to enter the room. "You were asking about Charlie, and here he is. May I present . . ."

"Hello, Chucky."

"Hello, Janie."

"Oh, I see you've already met. Won't you join us for a soda? Waiter, strawberry Nehis all 'round. Monsieur Charlie, mademoiselle here, she was asking about you earlier in a way that made me most jealous." Charlie adjusted his glasses nervously.

"I'm sure you weren't the same." Janie smiled.

"Let's see, the last time we met was at lunchtime, by the teeter-totters."

"How nice, you remembered."

"How could I forget. We traded sandwiches, your peanut butter for my tuna. You were wearing a sleeveless floral spring dress." Charlie raised his glass. "Here's look'n at you, kid."

"Oh, look at the time!" Wednesday offered a casual salute. "I don't mean to be rude, but it's past Janie's bedtime. May I call you a taxi, mon cheri?"

"Come again anytime, Miss Janie." Charlie stood up.

"Say goodnight to Sid for me."

"I will."

It was getting late at Café Americain; the once-bustling crowd dwindled to only a handful of die-hard customers. Charlie made his rounds, taking time to chat with patrons. Sid, the piano player, continued to sing and play softly in the background. Charlie raised the piano lid to verify the two precious hall passes. Distraught over painful memories of the past, Charlie pounded his fist on the table. "Of all the sarsaparilla joints in all the towns in all the world, she walks into mine!"

Sid continued to practice the piano.

"What's that you're play'n?"

"Oh, a little somethin' of my own."

"Well, stop it! You know what I want to hear."

Sid, perhaps in a misguided attempt to protect Janie, feigned ignorance. "Sorry boss, I don't."

Charlie became irritated. "You played it for her—you can play it for me."

"Well, I don't think I can remember . . ." Sid played a few false, off-key chords in an attempt to placate Charlie. Sid looked his boss in the eye—there was too much history between them. Sid was in the third grade, Charlie in the eighth; they'd known each other too well for too long.

"If she can stand it, I can! Play it!"

♫ *C-D-E, C-D-E* ♫

In the fog and rain of the bus stop, Charlie waited nervously with Janie. Janie felt like her heart was going to burst. There were so many things she wanted to say, yet she couldn't find the courage to put her feelings into words. Janie opened her mouth, tried to speak. She was about to say something, she really was, when the school bus pulled to the curb. The loud hiss of the air breaks put an end to the unbearable silence.

"Here's look'n at you, kid."

"Please, Chucky, do I haf'ta?"

"You sure do, kiddo, at least this time I know you won't be late for school." Charlie slipped Janie the precious hall passes and for a moment, their hands touched. "If that bus leaves and you're not on it, you'll regret it, maybe not today, maybe not tomorrow, but soon, and for the rest of your life. Listen, Janie, we'll always have Hartford. What we didn't have—we'd lost until you came to Casablanket. We got it back last night."

"When you said, 'I will never leave you . . .' "

"And I never will. I've got a job to do. Where I'm going you can't follow, what I've got to do you can't be any part of."

Captain Wednesday abruptly intervened. Insensitive to the emotions of the moment, Wednesday dumped Janie's leather strap-bound school books into her arms. As préfet and constable, Wednesday saw fit no other duty than to make certain Janie boarded the bus. Before the accordion doors closed, Janie paused and stole one last fleeting glance back at Charlie. "I love you."

Charlie never heard Janie's words; her small voice lost in the diesel's roar. The bus was gone. In the early dawn hours, Charlie and Captain Wednesday strolled off together across the wet pavement.

* * *

Where I'm going you can't follow, what I've got to do you can't be any part of.

The words repeated in Janie's head over and over, skipping like a scratched phonograph record . . . *Where I'm going you can't follow.*

"You're right, Chucky, except for one thing—I'm the one who's going."

Janie threw back her pillows, "Crud, fud, and fiddlesticks!" Janie didn't know any of what you might call real cuss words. For the first time, her mind was clear, her breast filled with a resolute resolve. She pulled up her white socks, put on her new saddle shoes, and chose her second-best sweater from the closet. She wrapped up the spam and cheese in a clean handkerchief and scraped the peas from the plate into the top dresser drawer where Mother would never find them.

* * *

Robert McConaughey unfurled his paper with a stiff snap befitting of a nineteenth-century sailing ship setting the top-gallant. The wall of paper served as an insulating factor and signaled the end to Saturday night supper. Paula continued to bustle in the kitchen; with a family of five, she never enjoyed a hot meal. The boys, John, Sidney, and little Robert Jr. were still finishing their dinner. Little Robert was squishing peas, John was excited about upcoming baseball tryouts, and Sidney announced he'd caught forty-two polliwogs in Hog River's pond.

"Sidney, you know how I don't like you going down to that pond alone!" Mother popped out of the kitchen brandishing a wooden spoon.

"Aw heck, Mom, Janie was in jail!"

"Your sister was not in jail!"

"Be quiet, Sidney." Robert crushed his paper. The conversation flagged and settled into an uneasy silence. While the grown-ups were preoccupied, pretending that everything was exactly as it should be, the children knew better. The unspoken word was: this was to be no different from any other family supper, but there was something different—a painful, noticeable difference. Where the usual six places were at the table, one place was conspicuously empty. It was as if someone were dead. Janie's chair sat empty, forlorn, and silent, (and Janie was never silent), a powerful testament to a family torn apart.

"More coffee, darling?"

"Thank you, my dear."

"The strawberries came in early this year." Paula brought to the table five dishes brimming with beautiful red berries and flakey biscuits. Paula was a West Virginia girl, and her homemade biscuits were a specialty. "There's no sugar."

"Ooh, Mommy made strawberry shortcake!" Little Robert bounced on his chair with such enthusiasm, he threatened to dislodge the Sears & Roebuck catalog used to boost him.

"I'm sure it will be fine. You're a wonder. I don't know how you do it with the war rationing." Robert stirred his coffee.

Paula held one extra dish of berries. "Bob, don't you think she's been up there long enough?"

Robert's irritation was choleric. "No, I do not! We're not going over this again— Janie is being punished!"

"I feel like the whole family is being punished. Please, Bob, strawberry shortcake is her favorite . . ." Paula was about to say something else when— "What was that?"

"It sounded like glass breaking."

Chapter 6

Down the Rabbit Hole

"Silly Daddy left his hammer behind."

"5, what have you done?"

"It did what you couldn't—wouldn't!" The villainous grendel hissed and spat. It turned towards its mistress and gnashed its yellow fangs. The anthropomorphic number ignored Janie's protestation to the contrary, and without the slightest care delivered a particularly savage blow. It continued to bash away at the window glass, "Don't be such a sissy pants all the time," 5 hissed, its breath was hot—yet it exhaled frost as if on a cold winter day.

"You should thank 5. You can do as you like, but 5 is leaving!" The nihilist thing bounded out onto the roof without regard to height or danger. "You'd better make up your mind, and quick!"

"Oh, gawd!" Janie was beside herself with anguish; her calamitous consternation was so complete she almost wet her pants. She was in big trouble. Her profound sense of panic only heightened with the rush of footsteps on the stairs. Daddy was coming and this time, she was sure to get a spanking!

The threat seemed real. The family legend and lore loomed large in Janie's mind, tales of boyhood terror, about trips to the woodshed, how granddaddy used to take her father and all her uncles out behind the woodshed and give 'em the strap. Janie dared a panicked assessment of her bedroom. Her two choices seemed clear: face her father and suffer the strap, or out the broken window and down the rabbit hole. She chose to egress the window.

Mother's rose bushes presented a formidable obstacle. Like German barbed wire . . . the Somme . . . France, 1916 . . . Janie drew her revolver and blew her squad whistle. She turned and beckoned Holly J. and Wednesday to follow her unto the breach, and over the top. Janie picked her way carefully across the treacherous, forbidding moonscape of no-man's-land.

The noble white oak tree grew quite close to the house. Mother hated it because in the fall it dropped acorns. Father loved it because it was the perfect anchor for a lazy summer hammock. Janie fancied it a perfectly lovely place to play. The broad, leafy canopy formed an idyllic home for squirrels and made the backyard quite shady and pleasant. One of the lower branches extended out and almost touched the roof. Father promised to cut it down, but like just about everything Father promised, he never managed to get around to it. The branch swayed in the light breeze, and with a friendly wave seemed to beckon and say, *Jump, I will catch you . . . Yeah, right.* When faced with the actual leap, the branch appeared very much farther away than before.

Teetering on the brink of the Mutier escarpment, Janie balked; a slight misstep caused a cascade of small stones to skitter over the edge and disappear from view. Her initial courage wilted away and was replaced by an interminable knot that formed in the pit of her stomach. The challenge was daunting as it was potentially dangerous, a twelve-foot drop to the ground. *Don't look down.* Janie thought she could do it. She had to do it!

The panicked parental shouts emanating from the broken bedroom window rekindled Janie's determination. She instantly discovered a wellspring of unknown courage she never knew existed. The way she figured it—if a prissy English girl like Jane Parker could swing from those vines in all those Tarzan movies, well, whatever she could do, Janie Firefly, jungle girl, could do better!

"Ooo aah ooh aah ee!" Janie dropped to the ground, pursued, nip-and-tuck, by a fearsome hoard of spear-wielding Maasai warriors.

"Oh, crud!" She'd torn her dress. *Where to?* Pitcairn Island, it seemed, was already taken. Janie Firefly, enemy of the people, political dissident, and escaped prisoner-of-war, could only think of one possible sanctuary: 625 Elm Street, Mr. Paradise's house. Unfortunately, Mr. Paradise lived on the farthest outskirts of Hartford.

Normally, she'd take the no. 2 bus to the end-of-the-line and walk the last two miles. Well, that wasn't going to work because she didn't have any money. Besides, they'd be looking for her for sure. Instead, Janie chose a different route; it amounted to a ten-mile hike. To get to the other side of town, she needed to cross the Hog River, which wasn't so much a river as it was a swamp, a morass of bogs, fiddle ferns, and estuaries. Janie knew the area well; they'd never find her there.

Chapter 7

Weary Willie

The morning sun was just beginning to peek out from behind the skyline that was C-town, Cleveland, Ohio. It was going to be another hot day, a scorcher, yet Bobby Segee felt cold. He tugged at his ragged jacket, drawing it tighter around his body to guard against the fresh breeze that blew off the southern shore of Lake Erie.

With no money, no purpose and no place to go, Bobby kicked a can around aimlessly. The last time he'd eaten was yesterday morning. He was sixteen years old, a high school drop-out, and not what the law considered a runaway. Not that it mattered all that much, it wasn't as if anyone was looking for him. Yet he had run away. He'd run away from his past, his pap, and the abuse that was his home in Hartford.

Bobby leaned up against the railhead and lit a cigarette, his last one. Cold and hungry in a strange place, in a strange town, he'd spent the last ten days riding the rails and dodging the railroad bulls, frequently falling prey to the older, more experienced hobos. His stomach rumbled. At first, he dismissed it as mere hunger pains, then a rumble shook his whole body, way deep down in his chest, followed by a far-off whistle.

A train was pulling into the station, a big train, too. Pulled by a great, black, belching Union Pacific 4-8-4 steam locomotive. The first few cars offered no clue, a water tender, a couple of coal cars. Then, there it was, a splash of color and a glint of gold. First, there were the air-conditioned animal cars, then came the flatcars, the boxcars, and finally, the luxury Pullman cars. It was a circus train. Not just any circus, it was the Ringling Bros. and Barnum & Bailey Circus: *The Greatest Show on Earth!* The circus had come to Cleveland.

For the first time, Bobby figured maybe his luck had changed. He watched as an army of roustabouts swarmed the rail yard. The unloading began even before the train had come to a complete halt. The big top alone amounted to over two acres of canvas with poles tall as a five-story building, and it all needed to be unloaded by noon if the circus was to make its two o'clock matinee.

Bobby Segee grimaced; his stomach growled. Oh how he hated work, but he hated being hungry more. He knew the circus was eager to hire local boys to serve as roustabouts. Manpower was in short supply, with most able-bodied men off either overseas serving in the military or working in factories. Segee was a big boy, strong for his age, and the circus train was his ticket for a hot meal. Bobby hopped down off the railhead and made his way straight to the canvas boss.

"How old are you, son?"

"Sixteen, boss."

Leonard Aylesworth chomped his cigar. The canvas boss remained skeptical, "What happened to yer face?"

"Nothin', boss, jest an accident." Segee did his best to dismiss the stinging scars where the crazy McConaughey girl had savaged his face. His hand slipped into his pocket. He felt the reassurance of the matches. He'd get even with that little bitch—someday for good!

"All raht, report to Whitey Versteeg, the stake boss on the north wall."

"I'm hungry Mr. Aylesworth, sir."

"You'll eat when we all eat!" Aylesworth snapped, "Now get to work!"

Unseen and unappreciated by the public was the intense coordination and manual labor required to erect a big top in six short hours. This was the greatest show on earth. There was one bulldozer, but even in the modern age, it was the elephants that provided most of the heavy lifting. With the poles secured, the canvas went up, and the circus made its two o'clock show.

The twelve-pound sledge whipped and thudded. Again, the hammers of the six-man sledge gang rose and eclipsed the sun. With each successive blow, the ash stake sunk deeper into the earth, and the one-inch braided sisal rope grew taut and then tightened to the point of twang.

Bobby Segee wasn't just strong for his age, his strength was prodigious. He was assigned work on a sledge gang. Six men worked in unison, driving stakes into the ground. It was a marvel of coordination and timing, a ballet performed with sledge hammers. It took some practice, but over the next six hours he proved he could swing a sledge with the best of the roustabouts. Bobby smacked the stake for a final time with such force that had it been a carnival high-striker, the blow would have sent the puck soaring and struck the gong.

Whitey Versteeg checked his watch before climbing down from the truck. He looked up at the sun, removed his fedora, and mopped his face. It was not yet nine o'clock and already the oppressive June heat shimmered in the air and dripped on the circus yard like hot candle wax.

"Hey, Segee! Git yer lazy ass over 'ere quick fer I kick yer can into Lake Erie!" The short-tempered roustabout boss was just as short in stature as he was short on praise. He was cautiously impressed with the new kid's strength, but he wasn't about to tell him. Besides, he'd thought of better use for the dumb kid's brawn: unloading five-gallon buckets off of the bed of the duce-and-half truck.

"Get over here, yah moron! And put that cigarette out!" Versteeg leaned over and popped the lid on one of the cans; the pail was full of a pasty white sludge. The noxious vapors were so strong that it nearly knocked Bobby's breath away.

"Smells like gasoline."

"That's 'cos it is, Einstein—gasoline and paraffin wax."

"Don't look like no gasoline I ever seen."

"It's called dope, yah dope, and you two ought to get along swell since you both have the same name." Versteeg tossed Bobby a push broom. "We had some rain last show in Pittsburgh, leaked all over the bandstand. Water run down the back of the second tuba. Mr. Healy was not happy. He said for me to fix it before the afternoon matinee. When he said *me*—that means *you*!" Versteeg gestured to a two-hundred-yard expanse of canvas. "It's easy, just like spreading manure. You do know how to spread shit, don't you, boy?"

"I reckon so, Mr. Versteeg." Bobby continued to puzzle as to the purpose of the strange concoction. "Still don't know what fer."

"That's 'cos you don't know everything. Waterproof'n. Now get this spread out quick so we can fly this canvas and make the show!"

Bobby dumped a pile of sludge onto the canvas and began pushing it around with a broom. His dim-witted brain continued to struggle to reconcile the particulars of the noxious gunk. "If this is waterproof'n like you sez . . . Shouldn't we be using rubber or something? Gas is kinda flammable 'n stuff, ain't it so Mr. Versteeg?"

"Why, you think'n of starting a fire, boy?" Versteeg laughed at his own joke. "Len Aylesworth told me you was some kind of retard, but you got some brains up there after all. Yeah, it's flammable alright, but there's a war on, can't get the good stuff.

It's safe enough, I reckon, circus folks been using this same dope for years."

* * *

"Hey, cookie, gimme some more of yer artillery!" Bobby Segee shoveled pork 'n beans and cornbread into his face until he thought he could eat no more. For a boy who just yesterday had led a shiftless life of nothing but petty theft and starvation, life was pretty goddamn good.

Bobby Segee lay under the stars. He'd earned two dollars, a meal, and a place to sleep. The morning breakfast of hotcakes and bacon was even more enticing. He pulled up the blanket, now his feet were cold. He couldn't get comfortable. A barking dog kept him awake.

"Flammable, huh?" Bobby sat up; the matches were still in his pocket. He felt a sanguine rush of heartless vengeance. He'd thought of his plan, a perfectly hellish, horrific plan.

* * *

Janie slogged through the muck and the mire that was Hog River swamp. With every passing hour, she felt more miserable and more dejected. Even though she'd played along the banks of the Hog River hundreds of times, she never remembered it being quite so muddy or mucky as this. The river, for whatever reason, was especially high, a boggy, murky, miry morass.

"Face it, angelface, you're lost!"

"Go away, 5!" Great! That's the last thing she needed. If she didn't have enough troubles already, now she had to contend with wicked 5 following her, taunting, teasing her every misstep. The malfeasant miscreation scampered on ahead.

"Good, it's gone." The nefarious thing wasn't gone, only hiding in the thicket. Janie discovered this too late when a branch smacked her in the face. The anthropomorphic number shrieked with laughter. Janie didn't think it was very funny at all—she rubbed the switch mark on her face.

"Yep, you're lost all right," 5 heckled. "What a dumb Dora! Ten days from now, I bet some do-gooder Boy Scout is gonna find a scrawny, spindly skeleton out here in these woods . . ."

♫ *The worms crawl in, the worms crawl out.*
All over the dead girl's nose and snout! ♫

The contemptible id was cruel as it was unrelenting. 5 continued its iniquitous taunt, "Skeleton-finding, yeah, that's what you are. You're noth'n but a merit badge in waiting!"

"Shut up, 5!" Janie was not so easily deterred. She pressed forward, but she was sincerely beginning to regret her decision to cross the Hog River. Only the distant wail of a police siren provided the impetus to propel her ever deeper into marshlands. *It's that fat wop goombah Ficano!* Janie struggled; the two-mile trek was turning into an ordeal. Apparently, Janie Firefly, jungle girl, she was not. Filthy, dirty, her white pinafore dress was ruined; not exactly the most practical outfit for slogging it out in the quagmire of Hog River. Gnats and mosquitoes buzzed her ears and feasted on her flesh. Her exposed arms and legs were savaged with briar scratches and bug bites. Janie took two steps and sunk into the mire up to her knees. The suction was so great it threatened to pull off her saddle shoes.

"Oh, fuck!" That was the first time Janie ever even thought that word—let alone said it out loud. It was a dirty word, and she knew it, even if she wasn't quite for sure what it meant. Absolutely, positively the dirtiest word known to all of kiddom—a word so forbidden, it practically guaranteed a trip to the bathroom and a destiny with the Lifebuoy soap. The cuss word represented a Rubicon of sorts; she was officially on her own. So much so, Janie almost wished there was someone there to punish her for saying it.

The summer afternoon light was fading, and she was nowhere near close to her destination. The prospect of spending the night in Hog River bog was fast becoming a reality. Everywhere she looked, there were long shadows. The dismal swamp was not only unappealing, it was frightening. Janie took a swat at a particularly vicious mosquito. Splat! She'd smacked her own cheek. Her hand came away bloody. *Catching polliwogs with her brother Sid never seemed this hard.*

The house lights dimmed, the monochromatic film rolled.

A hush fell over the crowd as the Republic logo, a majestic eagle perched atop a craggy mountain, appeared on the closed crimson curtains. The curtains swished and parted, the announcer intoned: "Come with me now on the amazing adventures of Janie Firefly and her sidekick, Wednesday the Wonder Girl!"

Republic pictures presents: The amazing new adventures of
Janie Firefly Staring Janie McConaughey as Janie Firefly
Shooting through the stratosphere
faster than a speeding bullet!
THRILL to Janie Firefly fighting to
save the world from destruction
as the evil Zerg-the-Nefarious unleashes his ultimate plot:
THE MOON-MEN-FROM-MARS
Next week, Chapter Two, THE MOLTEN TERROR!

Janie's foot was stuck fast in the suction that was the molten terror of the mud of Hog River swamp. "Oh, double fuck!" Never mind her white socks—she just wanted to retrieve her shoe. Her original plan was falling apart. It seemed so simple, cross the Hog River to Mr. Paradise's house where she was sure to find a warm bed, sausages, and strudel. Janie clambered up the embankment; briar, swamp, and thicket barricaded her on three sides. Janie sat down, dejected, just a hundred yards short of the no. 49 cutoff of the Penn Central track that cut through the swamp. She poured mud out of her shoe and scratched a mosquito bite. Tears welled in her eyes. *What am I going to do?* There on the gravel verge, swallowed by despair, she first felt a rumble, then heard the lonesome whistle wail.

Where I'm going you can't follow, what I've got to do you can't be any part of. The train was a blank slate. Mr. Paradise's house became a distant, forgotten memory. The train was a way out of this "fucking swamp." There, she'd said it again! Suddenly Janie's mind felt clear. She hadn't had a hallucination in the past half hour. She knew what to do. She had no idea where the train was going or where it would take her. She watched as the rows of boxcars of the Chesapeake & Ohio crept by, one at a time. They all looked about the same. *Which one to choose?* The open cargo doors beckoned her; it was a simple matter, even for one very small eleven-year-old girl, to hop a ride.

The forty-foot wagon-top boxcar jumped and jarred, the wheels ground round in a constant click and clack on the rails. The relentless bump and grind was so unrelenting, it reminded her of her brother's torturous *C-D-E.* The open-slat boxcar allowed for the last fading rays from the afternoon sun to waltz and play across the floor. The scintillating stripes of sunlight flickered and danced, then disappeared completely as the train passed beneath a bridge. Janie was plunged into utter and complete darkness, only to emerge as the fading rays of the afternoon sun flared and offered up a modicum of hope and comfort.

It was a cattle car. "Oh, crud!" Janie scraped her shoe. Was there anything else that could possibly go wrong today? Janie cloistered herself in the farthest, darkest recesses of the box-car; she drew up her knees tight under her chin and buried her face in her arms. Now was as good a time as any to cry.

An errant tin can pitched and skittered across the floor, dislodged by the rolling motion of the train. The sudden sound startled her. Janie jerked to alertness. "Hello, anybody there?" There was no answer; she was most definitely, positively alone, and in more ways than one.

"I never forget a face, but in your case, I'll be glad to make an exception." Charlie pantomimed knocking the ash off a cigar; Groucho Marx was his favorite comedian.

"Cut it out, Chucky!"

"Cut it out yourself. Cry'n don't suit you, kid—face all red and scrunched up like that."

"I got troubles."

"Jest try'n to cheer you up, that's all."

"Well, you can stop trying—I'm not in a funny mood."

"Jiminy Christmas! What in the Sam Hill are you do'n out here anyways? Ride'n the rails like you thought you was some kind of hobo or something."

"Oh, Chucky, I'm scared!"

"No need for that . . . My Uncle Nelson always said the farmer did his best pray'n at the bottom of the well."

"Stop it! You're mak'n fun of me. I can't go home on account 'cos if'n I do, Daddy's gonna wup the tar out of me. I can't go home anyways, I think I'm lost. Everything I do turns out wrong!"

"That's where you're wrong, kiddo, 'cos you ain't think'n straight. *Chutzpah,* kid, that's the one thing you got plenty of, chutzpah."

Janie crinkled her nose, "What's huts-pa?"

"Don't be so upidstay. Sass, spunk, nerve, spine, call it what you like, but whatever-it-is kid, you got it in spades!"

"I don't feel so brave."

"Who am I talk'n to here?" Charlie made his voice sound like a tough guy from the Bronx. "Do my eyes deceive me? I thought you was the famous Janie Firefly, jungle girl, lion tamer! Pshaw! Turns out you're noth'n but a wussy girl!"

"I do want to be a lion tamer," Janie sniffed and wiped her eyes on her sleeve because her dinner was still wrapped securely in her handkerchief. Her face brightened. "Honest, Chucky, do you really think I'm all that? I mean brave 'n stuff?"

"Aw, heck, you're the bravest kid I know! Hey, listen, I got a new joke for the act: A skeleton walks into a bar." At the mention of the act, Charlie had Janie's attention. "The skeleton says, (this is your part), hey bartender, gimme a beer and a mop!"

This time Janie laughed, but not for long. She felt a rumbly in her tumbly. She suddenly realized she was hungry, starving more like it.

"It will eat."

"Oh no, you don't!"

5 seethed and slavered, and retreated to a neutral corner where the avaricious number proceeded to gobble down Janie's dinner of spam and cheese. This was the last straw. "You give that right back!" Surprised, 5 screeched as one angry little girl collided in a full-body tackle. Janie punched and thrashed and rolled around on the deck of the freight car until, her frustration spent, she lay exhausted. 5 was gone, and Janie was left bruised and bloody, sobbing alone in the dark.

* * *

Cleveland, Ohio—Janie clambered down off the freight car that had been her home for two days. Gluttonous, greedy, yellow-eyed 5 had made off with her spam and cheese. Except for a drink pilfered during a brief water stop in Scranton, the poor child suffered with nothing to eat and less to drink for two days. She felt light-headed; her legs were wobbly. She was so hungry she almost wished she'd saved the peas! She took a long, luscious drink from the water fountain on the platform, hopped off the boardwalk, and began an aimless trek away from the rail yard towards a circle of trailers. She looked around; there was no sign of 5.

There, off in the distance, was a great din of men and machines. Something was being erected, constructed. Janie heard what she thought was an elephant, she'd remembered hearing them before on a radio program: *The Wonders of Africa.* There was a sudden great heave, and there before her rose a massive origami expanse of canvas topped with a flourish of an American flag. It was a circus big top. The circus had come to Cleveland, and she was there.

The Greatest Show on Earth had three principal star attractions. The first headliner was the high-wire dare-devil act of Karl Wallenda and his Flying Wallendas. The second was the great Alfred Court, the archetype lion tamer who dared enter the steel cage surrounded by wild animals with nothing but a whip and chair. Court, along with his protégé, May Kovar, were the greatest animal trainers of all time.

The third was a lonely, homely, unassuming little man. Janie found him sitting alone, hunched over a campfire beside a trailer. There were long-johns and assorted other sundry laundry flapping from a makeshift clothesline. You'd never have guessed it by looking at him but he was the Ringling Bros. highest-paid performer. Janie discovered the star attraction of The Greatest Show on Earth busy doing nothing more important than frying potatoes and sausages. He was a perfectly ordinary little man; not comic or funny at all. He always thought himself homely and chose to hide behind the solace of his clown make-up. He was a tragic figure, a tramp. His name was Emmett Kelly, Weary Willie—He was the most famous clown in the world.

The curl of campfire smoke made Janie's mouth water. She didn't know it, but she'd stumbled upon the outskirts of a circus camp. Janie licked her hand and combed her fingers through her hair, pulled up her socks, and did her best to brush the burrs from her dress. Janie knew she was attractive, on account everybody was always telling her: *What a pretty little girl she was.* Grams said it was on account she had bone structure. Janie did not know for sure what that was, but whatever-the-heck it was, she sure hoped she had good enough bone structure to find someone willing to feed her some supper.

"I sure could eat one of those sausages, mister," Janie said in her best sleepy, little-girl voice.

Kelly looked up from the pan of sizzling sausages and sized up one very small, very dirty wastrel visitor. "Why kid, are you hungry?"

Janie clutched her stomach. Her tummy growled so loudly she was sure the man could hear it. "I sure am, mister, I could eat a horse!"

The old man gave the skillet a shake; the aroma, sight, and sound of the sizzling sausages were so enticing that Janie was quite sure she was going to starve to death right then and there. Janie stood there, more than a little bit pathetic; she wiped her nose on her sleeve. Still, the old man offered her no food.

"And I sure could use some company. Aht, ah! Don't sit down. I didn't say you was invited yet. I don'ts feeds nobody lessen they's a good talker, are you a good talker?"

Preternaturally cheerful by nature, after two dismal days spent alone in a cattle car with only adversarial 5 for company, Janie was emotionally exhausted and unusually stoic. Janie nodded.

"See, that's what I'm talk'n about, nodd'n ain't talk'n. If you can't make better conversation than that, you'd best just run along!"

"Oh, please, sir, my daddy says I can talk the leg off a wooden Indian!"

"Can you now? What's your name, child? . . . No, no, don't tell me!" Emmett waved the girl off. He pressed his hand to his forehead as if he were trying to conjure a vision. "Let me guess. Mary?"

Janie shook her head.

"Sally?"

"No."

"Jane."

Janie was dumbfounded. "How'd you guess?"

"It's an old carnival trick a swami taught me once." Emmett gave the sausages a final shake and skewered them with a fork. "Have a seat, kid, two for you, and two for me." He scooped up a heaping side of potatoes.

Janie took the plate. "Oh, thank you, sir, I'm very hungry."

Emmett watched the girl eat. She was ravenous, starving. "I'm not so hungry, please take another."

"It's Janie . . ." Janie looked up, her face stuffed with delicious sausagey goodness. Never in her whole life had she ever tasted anything so good, well, neither had she ever been quite so hungry.

"Janie Firefly," Janie added as an afterthought. She finally found time between bites of food to study the old man's face. Her host was a circus performer, all right; the creases of his face were perpetually caked in a greasy white smear that no amount of scrubbing or cold cream could remove.

"Pleased to meet you, Janie Firefly." The clown and the little girl shook hands. "Janie, you can call me Em."

"Are you a real clown, mister?"

"Oh, I suppose you could say that, done a bit a clown'n here and there. Enough of that, tell me the truth, kid, are you a runaway?"

"Oh, no sir, I mean Mr. Em sir—there's no worry about that. I work for Mr. Ringling North." (This wasn't exactly a lie; Janie did spend all day last Saturday pasting circus posters).

Kelly considered this for a moment. "I got to be careful. Mr. Healy sends 'round these bulletins, fer us to keep a sharp eye out for runaways. There's lots o' kids look'n to run away 'n join the circus."

"Aw heck, I'm no runaway. I'm a lion tamer. Not only that, I play a puppet in my best friend Chucky's comedy act!"

"Well, don't that beat all!" Emmett slapped his knee and laughed.

"Hey, Em! What'cha think you're a do'n? Why aren't you in costume? Showtime in twenty minutes!"

The unknown ghostly visitant appeared from beyond the clothesline dressed in full clown frippery, ruffled collar, and pointed hat, his face painted brilliant white. His eyes were blocked out in a diamond domino mask, an appearance so garishly grotesque that he looked like an escapee from a *Pagliacci* opera. The apparition's sudden appearance startled Janie so much, she dropped her plate—she thought she was having another hallucination!

"Whoa! Didn't mean to scare you, little lady." The clown laughed, "What you got here, Em, another one of your hard-luck runaway orphans?"

"Not exactly . . . Bill Ding Jr., I'd like you to meet Janie Firefly, lion tamer."

"A lion tamer, huh?" Well, ol' Court is get'n a bit on in the years; I thought the Kovar girl was tak'n on his act. Bill turned to Emmett, and on the sly whispered loudly, "She's just about the dirtiest little lion tamer I ever laid eyes on!"

Janie was so embarrassed she wanted to crawl into a hole and die.

"I'll admit she is a bit on the rough side, but she'll clean up alright I reckon." Emmett's laugh was so affable that Janie realized she wasn't being made fun of.

"Bill Ding Jr., that's a funny name."

"Aw shucks, Bill Ding, that's just my clown name. All circus folk got stage names. My real name is Walter Sylvester. You can call me Uncle Walt. Pleased to meet you, little lady. What'cha gonna do with her, Em?"

"Haven't quite figured that out yet. Say, Walt, do you still have any of Eloise's old clothes from last summer? A dress or something we could put her in?"

"Mm, might have someth'n. Where you from, young lady?"

"Hartford."

"Ooh we man, you're sure a long way from home! She's a runaway, all right. You better let Mr. Healy know she's on the lot and quick!"

"Oh, please don't send me home!" Janie was beside herself with anguish. She could get no read off the white clown's painted face, so she pleaded with Emmett, who was busy with a mirror applying his signature sad-face hobo make-up.

"If you don't send me home, if you let me stay, I'll do my act for you. I can do it right now if you like."

Emmett raised a skeptical eyebrow. "Can you now?"

Janie crinkled her nose; her dimples framed her charming smile. She reached out and touched the clown's face. He did not cringe. She drew two fingers across his cheek, transferring just enough greasepaint. She smeared her eyebrows and drew two vertical lines down on either side of her chin. The two circus professionals looked on with interest.

"There's trouble at the mill, a woman fell into a lens grinder!" Janie was a natural. Her peculiar psychosis allowed her to slip seamlessly between straight man and puppet. Janie quirked and exercised her greasepaint eyebrows, now she was a wooden puppet.

". . . Dis-ASS-ter!"

The act continued, "Hello, fire department?" Janie panto-mimed ringing up an old-fashioned crank phone, "I want to report a fire."

"Where's the fire, miss?" (That was Charlie's part).

"It's in the kitchen."

"How do we get there?"

"You got a truck, don't you?"

The two men laughed, they really laughed. It wasn't just the corny jokes. The kid was amazing. Janie Firefly, lion tamer, was a funny girl.

"The kid's funny, Em, I think we should keep her. We're due to play Hartford in a week. We can get her back to her folks then. In the meantime, we can tell anyone who asks that she's my niece from Syracuse."

There was no time to worry about that now, the high-pitched strains of the steam calliope, the signature sound of the circus, signaled the beginning of the two o'clock show. Em-mett hurried to finish applying his make-up. He set the kettle on to boil and handed Janie a pail. "Tell you what, Honey, go fetch old Em some water over by the elephant trough. There's a basin, towel, and soap in the trailer. Walt here is going to see to something for you to wear. When I come back, I want you clean-as-a-whistle." Emmett donned his bowler hat and gave it a tap. "In the meantime—Walt and I got a show to do."

Chapter 8

Elephant Walk

The sun was high in the sky, well past its zenith. It was already fifteen minutes into the afternoon show, the mood sustained by the lively sounds of march music courtesy of Merle Evans and his band. The air hung thick with the smells of popcorn and cotton candy. The midway was mostly devoid of people, except for a trickle of late-comers and the usual ne'er-do-wells without tickets; most of the crowd had already made their way into the big top and settled in for what promised to be a spectacular show.

The big top was erected quite close to the water, with a dramatic view of the harbor. Only the tracks of the Penn Central railroad separated the lot from the shores of Lake Erie. The flags of the big top cracked and snapped. The fresh breeze that blew off the lake was cool on her face, and the occasional gust of wind blustered so strongly that Janie clutched the hem of her dress, less the sudden breeze billow her Sunday best.

In the back lot behind Municipal stadium, Janie skipped along gaily, swinging the tin pail. It was an ugly, beat-up, perfectly ordinary tin pail with an iron bail for a handle. The writing on the pail was faded and scratched, but Janie could read it clearly: Swift's Loin Minute Steaks, Swift Co. USA. The thought of steaks made Janie's mouth water. The world had been at war for practically as long as she could remember, and her family hadn't had beef since rationing began.

"You're go'n the wrong way, kid."

Janie stopped short, startled by the voice; her eyes darted behind. She thought for a second wicked 5 must be sneaking up on her, playing mischievous tricks on her. There was no one around. 5 was nowhere to be found. Janie caught herself almost wishing 5 would come around. Anything was better than this.

Janie missed her friends. Sure, Holly J. was a smart aleck and Wednesday was forever scheming and frequently got her into trouble, but still, she missed them. Her two very best friends in the whole world abandoned her. In a capricious act of disloyalty, at the last second, they'd refused to board the train. The train lurched around the curve. Her two friends receded into the distance, exactly where she left them beside the verge in the Hog River swamp. Janie was left alone. Only wicked 5 followed her to Cleveland. For two days, the number was nowhere to be seen. Not since she pounded the snot out of it. Janie allowed herself a bitter chuckle. If she'd known it was that easy, she wished she had socked 5 sooner!

Janie took two more steps. The bail on the pail squeaked.

"The elephant yard is over that-a-way."

"Did you say something?"

"Sure," the pail creaked. "I distinctly remember Emmett saying *take that pail and fetch some water from the elephant trough.* That's what I'm trying to tell you, kid, you're go'n the wrong way."

Janie stopped in her tracks. There was no one there. "If somebody's play'n tricks on me, it isn't funny!"

Janie took two more steps and stopped. "Not much of a . . ." The squeaky voice cut off the moment Janie quit walking. She looked at the pail suspiciously, jiggled the handle. "If you'd let me finish . . ." The girl dropped the pail and jumped back. The stupid pail just lay there on its side. Now she was thoroughly perplexed.

"This is so upidstay!" Janie picked up the pail and walked in the direction of the elephant house.

"So, what brings you to Cleveland, kid?" the pail creaked.

"Oh, so it was you the whole time!"

"Just me."

"A pail that talks," Janie stopped being astonished. In her world, these sorts of things happen all the time. "I never heard of a talking pail before. What's your name?"

"I don't have a name. I'm just a pail," the pail said.

"Well, it says on your side: Swift's Loin Minute Steaks. I think I'll call you Swift."

"That's great! I never had a name before, Swift will do just fine."

"How long have you been a talking pail?"

"Long time, I suppose. A tinsmith in Pennsylvania made me in 1898. I got sent to a cannery where they filled me with minute steaks. I sat on the shelf for the longest time. Just how I ended up in Cleveland under a circus wagon, I can't say. I only started talking after I got rusty."

Janie reached the elephant yard where two large cows were mulling about, picking up hay with their delicate trunks. Janie had never seen an elephant up close, only in pictures in Grams' *Book of Knowledge.* The animals were enormous, bigger than she ever imagined, she was fascinated with the magnificent creatures. They seemed so gentle, despite their size.

"Swift, what do you know about elephants?"

"Not much, I'm just a pail. A dipper told me once they like peanuts."

"Peanuts, huh." Janie's sharp eyes searched the circus yard. She spied a discarded bag of roasted peanuts. Unaware of the potential danger, she approached the largest cow and offered up a snack. The enormous pachyderm reached out and touched her hand with its delicate trunk. With a finesse that didn't seem possible, the animal used two finger-like proboscises to pick up the peanuts and place them in its mouth, crunching loudly, shells and all. The trunk returned and snuffled and searched Janie's hand for further delectable treats.

"Sorry, that's all there is. You're funny!"

The elephants were such a novelty that Janie completely lost all track of time, if Swift hadn't creaked to the contrary, it's doubtful the girl would have ever remembered why she came to the elephant yard in the first place.

"You're supposed to fill me with water, remember?"

Janie crinkled her nose, "Some other time, Swift." She thought about the basin and washrag waiting for her back at the trailer. No, that wouldn't do at all, she felt so itchy, dirty, and grimy, what she wanted was a real bath. Janie stole a quick glance around the circus yard. There was nobody around; she looked longingly at the deep tank. Janie didn't hesitate; she boldly kicked off her shoes, stripped down her dirty socks, and pulled her dress off over her head. In a flash, she stood in the circus back lot free as a jaybird, clad only in her white cotton camisole and underpants. Janie took a flying leap into the deep, dark water.

The water wasn't exactly freezing, thanks to the radiant heat of the scorching June sun, but the icy water was still cold enough to suck her breath away. She played porpoise, plunged her head under the water, and burst back to the surface, sputtering and spouting. She shook her hair like a shaggy dog, refreshed; she continued to scrub away the dirt, sorrow, and tears until at last, she felt squeaky clean.

"Hey, kid! What the heck do you think you're a-doing? Get oughta there, kid, before I call Mr. Healy!" Janie was so preoccupied with her bath she didn't notice the brown-faced Indian boy. The surprise was mutual; the boy, not much older than her—was just as startled to see her as she was him. After all, a half-naked girl splashing about in the elephant trough isn't a sight you see every day.

Janie was caught. Even though she was still wearing her unmentionables, she felt pretty gosh darn foolish swimming there in the elephant trough. Janie was so embarrassed she thought she was going to die! She wasn't about to climb out— not in her underwear, not in front of some strange boy. She didn't care who he called. Janie clung to the side of the tank with just her head showing.

"Didn't anybody ever tell you—it isn't polite to spy on a girl when she's taking a bath?"

"I wasn't spying, 'n besides, didn't anybody ever tell *you* this is an elephant trough, not a public bathtub!"

Janie's face was hot.

"Are you gonna git oughta there or not?"

"If you fetch me my dress 'n turn around, I might."

Janie splashed, hesitant to climb out. First, she wanted to make sure the boy wasn't trying to steal a peek. "There, you can turn around now."

Janie stood in front of the boy, sopping wet and bedraggled, but oh so satisfyingly clean. It had all been worth it.

"I'm still gonna call the superintendent!"

"You can call Frank D. Roosevelt for all I care, but you'd better not; I'm Janie Firefly, lion tamer! I'm a friend of Mr. Kelly!"

"You don't look like no lion tamer I ever saw."

"If you don't tell, I'll show you a trick-with-a-hole in it!" Janie picked up Swift, the loin steak pail. The pail's handle creaked. "See, it's a magic pail."

"What! That ain't no magic pail, it's nothing but a rusty ol' bucket!"

"Sure it is, and it talks, too! What's your name, anyway?"

"Aarti . . . is that really a magic pail?" Aarti was just curious enough, naïve enough, and Janie's showmanship was persuasive enough, well, it could be a magic pail.

"Hello Aarti, I'm Swift, the magic pail." The pail squeaked. Janie threw her voice just like Charlie had taught her. The poor Hindi boy was as flabbergasted as he was amazed.

"Accha!"

"I'd better go. My daddy says I'm not supposed to talk to colored people."

"I'm not colored, I'm Indian!"

"Is that like an *Algonquian* or *Pequot*or sump'tin?" Janie studied Native American tribes of Connecticut in school. "I thought Indians were red?"

"You sure are a stupid, even for an American girl! I'm Indian, from Bombay. You do know where that is, don't you?"

"Of course, I do." Janie put on a huff. The boy called her stupid. "I'm leaving."

"Please don't go. If you don't go, I'll give you a ride on one of the elephants."

"Really, Aarti?" Now it was Janie's turn to be amazed.

"Sure, I'm a bullman, and these are my elephants."

The offer was too good to pass up. Janie imagined herself riding in a howdah in the jungles of India, stalking tigers. She quickly forgot all about the boy calling her stupid. "Oh boy, that would be swell!" Janie's eyes were smiling. Emmett returned to his trailer to find the dishes done, the floor swept, and Janie Firefly snoring softly, fast asleep in the top bunk, dreaming of elephant rides.

* * *

Janie did her best to sit still and not fidget while Uncle Walt applied gobs of greasy, pasty paint to her face. She'd been sitting on the chair for the longest time. The eleven-year-old's attention span was beginning to flag, and she found it darn near impossible not to squirm a teensy-weensy bit.

"Hold still, kid, we're almost done." Walt blackened her eyebrows, and with a grease pencil, he expertly crafted a dummy's chin, exaggerated rosy cheeks and scarlet lips completed her make-up. Walt turned the mirror around so Janie could see her face. The face that stared back at her was not her own. She was another person.

"Still needs work, but that will do for now. What-do-ya-think, kid?"

Janie was speechless.

"If you're gonna live with us in clown alley, you have to be one of us." Uncle Walt was a whole lot less scary without his clown make-up on. Walter was tall and lanky, with long arms and even longer legs, which made his movements seem unco-ordinated and awkward, a misperception he proffered to great comic effect. Walter was a very good dancer and got his start in show business as a hoofer in vaudeville.

"There are three kinds of clowns: the white, the *auguste,* and the elegant. Clowning is an ancient profession, goes way back to before medieval times when the harlequins wore make-up so they could behave rudely in front of the king and not get their heads chopped off! . . .Tsk!" Walter made an "off-with-their-heads" gesture so dramatic it made Janie jump.

"What kind of clown am I?"

"You're like me, a white clown, the comic." Walter fitted Janie with a blonde wig with tightly plaited pigtails. "Now you look the part!"

"Do something with the nose, Walt." Emmett looked on with interest. "She's supposed to be made of wood, something like Pinocchio."

"Hmm, so she is, let's see." Walter rolled some putty around in his hand, and after some trial and error, sculpted a silly nose.

"There we are, my little charlatan." Walt stuck a green leaf in the end of Janie's false nose as if she had just told a lie.

"She's perfect."

"Uncle Walt, what's a *Charlie-tan?*"

Walter smiled, "What-do-yah-think, kid?"

"It's upidstay."

* * *

Janie took a timid first step onto the plywood scaffolding; the sights and sounds of the crowd immediately buffeted her. The atmosphere was charged with excitement. She felt more than a little awkward, self-conscious in her Alpine miss costume and blonde Gretel pigtails. What if she made a mistake? This was nothing like rehearsal. Uncle Walt and Emmett assured her she was a natural. This was her first time in front of a big crowd and suddenly, Janie felt anything but natural.

Ringmaster Fred Branda's voice boomed over the PA, amidst the swish and swirl of the stark klieg spotlights. Merle Evans and the band struck up a lively rendition of, *"There'll Be a Hot Time in the Old Town Tonight."* That was her cue. Janie poked her head out of the fourth-story window of a cartoon house. Dry ice created smoke, and fake cellophane flames flickered under the houselights. Six-thousand eyes were upon her.

"Help! Someone save me!" That was her line—not much of a part to be sure—but Janie figured this was her first time out in show business, and she certainly had plenty of time to work up to playing *Anna Karenina* or *Lady Macbeth*. She made the best of it— and screamed and hollered for all she was worth. The crowd roared with laughter at the antics of the silly puppet-girl in peril.

All eyes turned towards the performer's entrance as a ridiculously tiny fire engine, piled high with clowns, sped around the hippodrome track. The speeding fire engine came to a sudden stop, and Bill Ding did an acrobatic somersault flip over the steering wheel while Sparkles, the tillerman, tumbled off the back end.

Janie laughed. *"You're not supposed to laugh, upidstay,"* Charlie had reminded her. Down below in the center ring, the clowns ran around in panicked circles in the Ringling Bros. interpretation of a Chinese fire drill. Instead of attacking the flames, the clowns sprayed each other with fire hoses and threw buckets of confetti into the audience. The crowd shrieked with laughter. The last gag of the program called for Bill Ding and his band of Keystone firemen to spread out a rescue net to catch the poor Alpine miss. The crowd began a rhythmic chant "Jump, jump!"

There was one last burst of pyrotechnics. Now comes the hard part, Janie thought. She closed her eyes and jumped, hoping against hope to land in the net. Instead, she bounced once, rolled off the net, and landed miserably, face-first in the sawdust. Not only did the clowns fail to catch the silly wooden fräulein, in the bungled confusion, they managed to set themselves on fire. The program was finished. The band played the traditional romp, *"Happy Days Are Here Again."* Bill Ding and the rest of the Keystone clowns ran out of the ring. Janie was supposed to follow behind. Instead of following the script, the wooden puppet-girl turned around, curtsied, and made a comic face for the crowd. Janie Firefly was a star.

* * *

From behind the bleachers, underneath the grandstand, Bobby Segee watched and waited. He'd dropped a spotlight during the morning rigging and Mr. Versteeg, the stake boss, berated him, smacked his face, and humiliated him in front of the other roustabouts. He watched the burning house program. The sight of the comic fire excited him on a sinister level. He took out the matches and struck a flame.

"Maybe just a little one—that'll teach them a lesson they'll never forget!" The fire began life as a flicker and a whiff of sulfur. Bobby watched with sexual fascination as the tiny flame took light, sputtered, and began to devour the sisal guy rope with hellish anticipation. The fire crept rapidly toward the real source of fuel, the tent curtain wall. An alert seatman quickly extinguished the flames and because no damage was done, decided not to report the incident to the superintendent.

Bobby grimaced, and ducked behind the flap, his anger piqued; his phlogiston progeny was extinct. He still had two more matches. The matches the Red Man gave him, the hellish nightmare which visited his dreams; the revenant who bade him to set fires. "Maybe next time."

* * *

"I'm tell'n you, Em, we ain't using her right. The kid is a natural. Did you see the way the crowd reacted to her last night?" Walter was just a little bit drunk. "I saw. I still say we give her twenty bucks and put her on a bus to Hartford. It's the right thing to do—her folks must be worried sick about her."

"We'll be in Hartford in six days. What's the hurry? In the meantime, we're sitting on a gold mine! The kid has talent. She could be the next Baby Peggy or Shirley Temple!"

"A gold mine is nothing but a hole in the ground with a liar at the bottom."

"Let the kid decide. Janie, come out here, I know you can hear."

Janie sat on the edge of the bunk, behind a makeshift camp table, eating a bowl of cornflakes. She always ate cornflakes fast because she liked them best while they were crunchy, and you only had a couple of minutes before the delicious yellowy flakes of corn turned into mush city. She poured another bowl; she was still hungry. It was canned milk. Walter called it "armored heifer," that made Janie laugh. Canned or not, just having all the milk she wanted to drink was a novelty all by itself. She was about to set a new world record—when she realized she hadn't taken a bite for five minutes. Her spoon hovered halfway between the bowl and her mouth. She wasn't exactly eavesdropping, but it was impossible not to hear the two men on the other side of the curtain arguing her fate. She took a tepid bite. "Yuck, mush!"

"Janie, come out here." The curtain that divided the caravan between the kitchenette and the bunk beds parted, it was Uncle Walt. "You did good last night, kid, real good. I'm proud of you."

Janie rubbed her nose where she banged her face on the floor after getting dumped off the safety net.

"Aw, just a bump and a grind, it's part of the trade. You'll get used to it after a while. Listen to your Uncle Walt. Do you want to be a real performer? I found this for you to use from the prop wagon." Walter plunked down an enormous cartoon telephone. "Do that business you did for us the other day, the joke where there's a fire in the kitchen."

Janie's eyes were as big as saucers. The phone was ridiculously large. She suddenly felt foolish and self-conscious.

Emmett wasn't convinced. "Still feels like kidnapping."

"Why do you have to go and spoil everything all the time? There's no kidnapping to it—the kid is a runaway. We're just a couple of good-hearted souls tak'n care of her, that's all—least until we make Hartford." Walter was obstinate. "Besides, I got it all figured out. We get the prop men to knock together a kitchen set, stove, table, maybe a big mixing bowl with some goopy-gloppy batter. We can put in a bit where she's stirring, slopping, dumping in flour, regular slapstick stuff. The kid is baking a cake . . ." Walter, preoccupied with his brainstorm, failed to notice Janie's bother every time he called her 'The kid.'

"Janie Firefly, I'm not the kid!" Janie interrupted.

Walter squinted, took another drink of whiskey, chastened by a girl! He cleared his throat. "Our bossy little miss here puts the cake in the oven. Two seconds later, the oven starts to smoke . . . When she sticks her head in the oven, boom, the oven explodes! The kid here comes out all splattered in cake batter and blackface! You know how the locals love darkie jokes. Lots of smoke 'n fake flames, that's when the kid does her fire-in-the-kitchen business. Me 'n the Keystone boys come roar'n to the rescue just like last night. Brilliant, huh?"

"It's funny, Walt, but I still think we're better off putting her on a bus."

"No jumping out of windows?" Janie rubbed her nose again. She decided if she was going to be world-famous, she most definitely, positively needed a *No Jumping Out of Windows* clause in her next contract.

"No windows, kid, you'll get to tell your joke in front of six-thousand people! Do you think you can do that?"

"Of course, I can."

Chapter 9

Ladies and Gentlemen

The ringmaster was part shill, part promoter, and most important of all, master of ceremonies. It was his job to keep the performers on their toes and the pace of the show to a brisk two hours and twenty minutes. Fred Branda was the only ringmaster the Ringling Bros. show had known for the past eleven years. An artiste himself, Branda began his career with the circus as an equestrian performer, and later equestrian director before donning the top hat, coat and tails and stepping into the center ring.

Of all the many hats the ringmaster must wear, and Branda would tell you this himself if you asked, it was to create a sense of excitement, a well-rehearsed ballyhoo of aggrandizement and hyperbole when introducing the acts. Branda did it better than anyone with his over-the-top declarations of: *amazing, spectacular, and spellbinding!*

"Ladies and gentlemen, boys and girls, children of all ages . . . Welcome to the most extravagant extravaganza in entertainment history! Ringling Bros. and Barnum & Bailey Circus is proud to present: The Greatest Show on Earth! May I direct your attention now to the center ring—let's have a big round of applause for the star attraction of tonight's show, the amazing, spectacular, spellbinding, Janie Firefly, lion tamer!"

* * *

". . . Of course, I can."

"That's my girl!" Walter rummaged around in Emmett's icebox for a carton of eggs. He never bothered to ask or nothing. He searched the cupboard for a mixing bowl and egg beater.

"What's for breakfast?"

"You, kid, are going to learn how to juggle. I hope you learn fast 'cos this is what you're going to do tonight. I'm going to show you how to toss juggle. It's the most basic form of juggling. Now watch close." Walter held up three eggs. Janie watched in amazement as the clown tossed and caught the eggs. The eggs whirled in mid-air in perfect synchronization. Walt cracked the first egg, the second, and he let the third plunk into the bowl, shell-and-all for comic effect. He mixed the eggs vigorously with the egg beater and made a silly face. "That's called business, kid, now you try."

"Do you think I can?" Janie frowned. Uncle Walt made it look so easy.

". . . I'll get the broom," Emmett said, "Maybe we should try some rubber balls first and work up to the eggs?"

"Takes practice, you keep at it."

After lunch, and only a few dropped eggs later, Janie had the juggling part down pat. "What did I tell you Em, the kid is a natural. Now let's try the egg beater."

Janie cranked the egg beater enthusiastically, just as Uncle Walt had done. To her chagrin, egg batter flew all over Emmett's tiny kitchen. What a mess! Janie had egg in her hair; egg on her face. The two clowns laughed uproariously. It was all a setup. Walter thought it a great joke. Janie didn't think it was funny at all. She scrunched up her face, no, she wasn't going to cry, but she sure felt like it! This clowning stuff was a whole lot harder than it looked.

"Hey, what's with the sad face, nothing to get all worked up about. See, it's a gag egg beater, here let me show you." Walt patiently took Janie's hands and showed her how to work the egg beater. "Turn the crank backwards to mix the eggs, turn it forward, and the darn thing throws eggs everywhere! It's supposed to do that, kid. It's a prop. You practice some more, Em and I have a two o'clock. When we get back, we'll work on your make-up."

It was decided to go with a more natural look. Janie was far too pretty, too charismatic to remain hidden under a mask of heavy stage make-up. Gone were the Gretel pigtails and caricature Pinocchio nose. In place of the ugly putty nose, Walt drew a delicate rose-bud form with a ruddy grease pencil. Edith White, the costume lady, made her an enormous tilted red flannel hair tie in the shape of a bow.

"She'd be a whole lot prettier if her hair were longer." Mrs. White frowned. "Such a shame. That short hair makes her look like a little Dutch boy," the costume lady said without thinking. "Who cut your hair, child?"

Mrs. White called her a boy! Janie fumed—grown-ups can be so rude. Don't they think little kids have feelings? She finally remembered her manners and said as if she didn't care, "Oh, that was my friend Wednesday."

* * *

The following evening performance was set for Thursday, Janie's big debut. Her name even appeared in teeny-tiny letters on the program. The big top echoed with the sounds of carpenters rushing to make last-minute alterations to the set. The center ring was forty-two feet in diameter. The center pole soared to a staggering height of sixty feet. The cavernous tent seemed so empty without the crowds, even the sounds of the rowdy roustabouts putting the finishing touches on the lights and rigging failed to fill the hollow amphitheater.

"Get a load of the little First of May!" Sparkles, the dwarf, toddled over to where Janie and Walter were rehearsing. "You gotta be kidd'n me. This is the new Kinker? She's shorter than I am!" A 'Kinker,' that was circus slang for any performer. Janie already knew that. She was smart enough to know when she was being insulted.

"Go do something useful, Sparks, like jump off a bridge." Walter was busy walking Janie through tonight's spec; there were a million little details.

"Ha-ha, very funny, I'll make the jokes around here; it's your job just to laugh at 'em. I'm just say'n if the kid fucks up, it makes us all look bad—and there's nothing I hate worse than look'n bad in front of the rubes." Sparkles played the tillerman on the Keystone fire brigade and was full of his own self-importance.

"Git oughta here! I ought'a smack your puss, and watch your language in front of the kid!"

"Uncle Walt, what's the First of May?"

"That's just circus talk for any new performer, see we start our season on the first of May. You just never mind about that, Sparks didn't mean nothing by it." Janie wasn't paying attention; how could she? May Kovar entered the steel cage and began rehearsal with the big cats.

"Whatever you do kid, when you stick your head in that oven, remember to keep your mouth shut. For a chatterbox like you—that's going to be the real challenge!"

Janie stuck out her tongue.

"Remember, mouth shut," Walter put his finger across Janie's lips. "Or you'll get a nasty surprise."

Janie was nervous enough already without that catty midget coming 'round and making fun of her! She didn't know why she was so nervous, after all, this was exactly what she wanted. She remembered the last time she got exactly what she wanted. She ate three ice cream sundaes at the Lincoln Dairy and got an upset tummy, too! Grams reminded her gently to be careful what you wish for because you just might get it. Now her tummy was upset for an entirely different reason. She most definitely, positively didn't like the idea of something exploding in her face! Walter reassured her; it was no worse than getting hit in the face with a water balloon. Somehow, Janie remained unconvinced; she'd wondered if there wasn't time enough to rescind her *No Jumping Out of Windows* clause in her contract.

The spec went off without a hitch. Janie dead-panned her fire-in-the-kitchen joke. The crowd roared with laughter at the antics of the silly puppet-girl. With the spec finished, Walter took Janie by the hand and led her to the edge of the ring; he bowed and nudged her to do the same. Janie curtsied like a true débutante and yucked it up for the crowd. Sparkles the dwarf ran over and presented Janie with a bouquet of red roses, and a lemon meringue pie for Walter. Everyone, it seemed, everyone except Janie, knew exactly what was coming next. Walter smacked Janie in the face with the pie! Baptism by custard; her mouth was open and everything! The gag was of such monumental, stupendous surprise, at first the girl was in shock. Judging from the roar of applause, they were clapping for her! Janie Firefly took a bow. "Welcome to the circus, kid!"

* * *

High atop the blue bleachers, in a row of unsold seats, Bobby Segee leaned back and watched the performance unfold with interest. In another forty-five minutes, the show would end, the crowds go home, and the real work would begin. That's when that short little prick Versteeg would come 'round and start barking orders for the frantic rush to tear down the big top and get everything loaded onto the train for the midnight run to Reading.

Bobby tossed popcorn in the air, only catching about half the kernels. He drank a warm soda he'd found discarded in a trash bin as he watched the stupid little puppet-girl get smacked in the face with a pie. He laughed a vulgar laugh. Oh, how she deserved it!

There was something vaguely troubling about that custard-face girl. Her voice; he tried to place that voice, that lilting sing-song voice burned in his brain. Bobby was never bright enough to qualify for an epiphany or any other kind of intuitive leap of understanding, but on a primitive level, his dim-witted brain managed to connect-the-dots. He knew where he'd heard that voice before!

"Bobby Segee is a bologna butt!"

It was her, he just knew it! Oh, how he hated that girl! So wrapped up was he in his thoughts of vengeance—he never even bothered to consider the amazing coincidence as to what twist of fate brought them both here to Cleveland. He only needed ten minutes. Ten minutes alone with that girl, and he'd teach her a lesson she'd never forget! The little bitch wouldn't have time to forget. Bobby allowed himself a cruel laugh because by the time he finished—she'd be dead!

"Welcome to the circus, Janie McConaughey."

Chapter 10

Hôtel du Quai

At eleven o'clock, the flag on the cookhouse went up.

"Wake up, sleepyhead."

"Breakfast time already?" Janie rolled over, rubbed her eyes, and sat up on one elbow. This wasn't Emmett's trailer. It was a Pullman berth. She had fallen asleep the night before with the sound of applause in her ears and slept so soundly that when the whistle called all aboard, Walt and Emmett didn't have the heart to wake her. They bundled her up in a blanket and trundled her on a sleeping berth for the midnight jump to Reading, Pennsylvania. Except they weren't in Reading; they were stuck in some Podunk town; nobody was quite sure where. In the middle of the night, the circus train was diverted and stalled on a siding by priority army trains. It was going to be an all-day wait. The decision was made to set up the cookhouse and feed the crew and animals alike.

"You darn near missed breakfast, kiddo! Your Uncle Walt is taking you to a real swanky joint, noth'n but the best for my little dilly girl."

"Where are we going?"

"The *Hôtel du Quai*," Walt joked in his best fake French accent.

"Hotel do key?" Janie was still sleepy. She thought maybe she heard wrong. Janie sat up on the edge of the bed and dangled her legs over the side of the berth.

"Dukie, that's lunch to you, kid. Com'on, get dressed. We got all day to goof off, and you're my date."

Janie pulled her dress on over her head; her elbow tore through the sleeve.

"Oh, crud!"

Walter chuckled, "Looks like somebody needs to go see the *Monday Man*. Get you some new clothes, kid."

Janie puzzled.

"Wash day is Monday. Abe, he'll find you something to wear even if he has to swipe it off the wash lines of one of the locals. Now hurry up!"

The cookhouse tables were set with red-checkered table-cloths and white crockery. The cook staff was hard at work; the air was full of the delicious smells of frying pork chops, and piles of bacon, eggs, and toast. Janie was hungry.

"How this for eats, sweetheart?"

"Helloo, Aarti!" Janie hollered across the bustle of the dining room. Her friend Aarti was having his own breakfast with the other bullmen, and a man she assumed must be his father. He had the same copper-black skin, and he wore a turban. Aarti either didn't hear or did his best not to. Aarti heard. Oh bother! It was that crazy naked girl, the one with the talking pail!

There was a defiant hierarchy in the circus. The roustabouts and cageboys ate at their own tables, separate from the bally girls. Janie ate with the clowns, aerialists, and acrobats. Some of the headliner performers, like Court and the Wallendas, never ventured from their private staterooms. Emmett's trailer was on the flying squadron, a truck somewhere between here and Reading, so he ate in the tent along with the other clowns. Walter never cottoned up to all that uppity stuff and took his meals in the cookhouse.

Sparkles was making an ass of himself, as usual, molesting the bally girls and irritating almost everybody. "What you bash'n there duchess, gimme a buzz sweetcakes." Sparkles tried to steal a kiss from Tillie.

"Get your paws off me, short stuff!" The bally girl screamed and shoved Sparkles off her lap.

Janie was busy buttering her toast.

"How 'bout some lemon meringue pie, angelface?" Janie cringed, angelface! The name brought back a zillion bad memories. The same name nasty 5 called her! This time it wasn't 5—replaced instead by someone equally insufferable, that fathead dwarf! Janie groaned; the joke may have been funny when Uncle Walt did it—but she really didn't feel like putting up with Sparkles and his shenanigans at breakfast. Just her luck, if she didn't have wicked 5 pestering her—now she had to contend with someone equally obnoxious.

"Oh, isn't she just the most adorable little ol' thang?" Tillie came to her rescue and squeezed her cheeks like a long-lost aunt.

Janie never saw Bobby Segee come into the cookhouse, uncouth and jostling with the rest of the rowdy roustabouts. Unlike Janie, who enjoyed special privileges as the guest one of the circuses' most important performers, the roustabouts traveled with the circus, relegated to makeshift quarters in converted cattle cars.

"What's a matter there, Bobby boy, ain't you hungry? Me'n the boys are think'n of head'n into town fer a little alcomahol 'n recreation. Maybe hook up with a couple 'o shebas. Fer a fin you can get your pole greased. What-do-ya-say?"

Bobby didn't have five dollars.

Bobby saw her, and this time with no make-up. Something soured in his stomach. His filthy eyes followed her as the girl finished her breakfast and got up and left, laughing with the clown. She wouldn't be laughing for long.

* * *

The circus train pulled into Reading late that afternoon, too late to set up for the evening performance. The whole date was a wash, and Mr. Healy, the vice-president of operations, was furious. There was a rush to set up the big top and salvage what they could for tomorrow's show. The next morning there was an extra-special, spectacular parade. Main Street was filled with the sight and sound of elephants and the shrill refrain of the steam calliope. There were hundreds of clowns, bally girls, and a marching band. It was all so grand, so very exciting! This was Janie's first circus parade ever, and she was in it! She got to ride on one of the brightly-colored wagons, wave to the cheering crowd, and yuck it up with Walt and the other clowns. The Greatest Show on Earth was in town, and Mr. Healy made certain the good folks of Reading didn't forget!

After the two o'clock performance, Janie found time to wander over to the elephant yard where she was eager to catch up with her friend, Aarti. She was just a little provoked; she suspected the Hindi boy of giving her the short shrift.

"Hey Aarti, why so high-hat? I thought we was friends? Didn't you hear me when I hollered?"

"I heard. What do you know about the circus? You're nothing but a dumb girl who doesn't know noth'n 'bout nothing. You never fired-off-a-cannon or shot-off-a-hand-sled. I'm a cageboy—you're with the clowns. Zanies and the animal people don't mix."

"I thought you said you was a bullman?"

"Naw, I'm not a real bullman. I mostly just feed the elephants and the rest of the hay burners and shovel poop. Yep, I shovel poop. Elephants poop a lot!"

"Was that your father, the man I saw you with, the one with the turban?"

Aarti's face brightened, "My father is a bullman! Timba, he's our elephant. He's the largest Indian elephant in the show!"

"Do you still want to mess around?"

"Sure, let's go down to the midway and see if we can get a free hot dog."

"Git lost, kids!" The concessionaire was not in a charitable mood.

"Crud! I sure'd like a drink of orangeade."

"Com'on, Janie, I know how we can get some money. Let's sneak under the sidewall and see if we can scrounge up some soda bottles dropped under the grandstand."

The plan sounded familiar. The confined space under the bleachers was a dark maze of struts, stay cables, and lattice-work, just the sort of place that in the past would have triggered a wild fantasy. Janie's mind remained clear; she was most definitely, positively under the bleachers, and nowhere else so fantastic. The search for soda bottles yielded one nickel, six Coke bottles, and two Nehis, and the biggest prize of all, a Dr. Pepper with the crown cap still intact!

"Pull left, you goddamn moron! When I say left, I mean your other left!" Whitey Versteeg screamed obscenities and chased after the stupid boy with a stick. Janie peeked out from between the bleachers to see what all the commotion was about.

This time *she* saw *him*! Hoisting on a rope with a gang of roustabouts, the last time she'd seen him was in the vacant lot behind Quigley's hardware. She remembered being on top of him, punching him, pummeling him. Sheriff Ficano said she bit him, although she had no specific recollection, she knew what viciousness 5 was capable of—and there was no doubt the boy was pissed.

"Oh, fuck!" This time the dirty word didn't slip out, she said it on purpose. Janie figured she was getting pretty good at this cussing. Of course, never before in her whole life did she have so many dire troubles where crud, fud, or fiddlesticks simply failed to convey her unimaginable anxiety.

"We got to get oughta here!"

"We ain't finished get'n the bottles yet." Aarti objected.

"I'm finished, and keep your voice down! Are you com'n or not?"

Janie wormed her way underneath the sidewall without the slightest care if Aarti followed her or not. She was in big trouble! This was a catastrophe! What was she going to do now? How in the heck did he get here? She had the presence of mind to pull up her socks and smooth her dress where it got all scrunched up from crawling around on her hands and knees. She realized she was shaking.

The two children exited near the steel chute that led to the big cat cages. The lion roared and lashed out between the bars.

"Accha! It's Léonide, he mauled one of Court's trainers last year in Pittsburgh!"

"What?" Janie wasn't listening; she was rattled by her encounter with Bobby Segee.

"Look at the size of those paws! Hey Janie, you said you was a lion tamer. I dare you to open the cage, 'n do sumpt'n with those lions."

Janie felt a second knot twist in her stomach. "Oh, I never exactly trained with these lions . . ."

"I just knew you was full of beans! You can't fool me—you're nothing but a big fat liar! Go on, I double-dare you!"

"All right, I will."

"Hey, kid, get down from there! Do you want to get yourself killed?" It was the man himself: the great Alfred Court, dressed in khakis, pith helmet, and everything! "I ought to tan your hide! He pulled Janie off the side of the animal cage. Before he sat her down, he gave her a firm swat on the behind.

"I just wanted to see the lions."

"In another two seconds, you'd been look'n at angels. That was a very foolish thing to do. Those are wild animals. They're dangerous! If I ever catch you fool'n around these animal cages again, young lady, you'll get worse than that! Do you understand?"

"Yes sir . . . are you Mr. Court?"

"You're just lucky ol' Léon here doesn't have any teeth." Janie and Aarti watched in dumbfounded amazement as the great man stuck his whole arm in the lion's mouth to prove his point. "I can do that because I've been doing this for thirty years. You two ankle-biters run along, skedaddle! Before I call the law!" The two children didn't have to be told twice, they ran fast as they could back to the elephant yard.

"Aarti, wait up!" Janie was out of breath. "If I told you sumpt'n, you wouldn't make fun of me or noth'n?" The girl bit her lip; the time came for the truth. "My name is Janie McConaughey, and I'm not really a . . ."

"It's okay, Janie. I know. I'm not really a bullman, either."

* * *

"Get in the chair kid, time for your make-up."

"Uncle Walt, I don't want to do the show tonight."

"What's bothering you, kiddo? Sophomore jitters? The entrée is the same as this afternoon. You'll do fine."

"I just don't want to, that's all. I want to go home."

"What's the matter?" Emmett asked.

"Our little lightning bug doesn't want to go on." Walter's voice betrayed a hint of irritation that Janie had never heard before. "She says she wants to go home!"

"We can't keep her here—if Janie wants to go home, we put her on a bus, tonight. I told you what to do four days ago."

"You're just homesick, kid. That's all. Don't you like living here with your Uncle Walt and Em?"

"Oh no, it's nothing like that. I like it just fine. You guys have been swell—the best friends I ever had! It's just I'm scared."

"Did something happen? Is Sparks giving you the business again? I just knew it! I'm gonna kick that bastard's can!"

"Something happened—there's this thing you don't know about me. I'm a bad girl. I do bad things. 5 is gonna come back and do something awful. I just know it!" Janie began to sob.

"Who's five?"

"Uncle Walt, when you was a little kid, were you ever afraid of monsters in the dark?"

"I suppose every kid is afraid of something now and then. When I was your age, I used to be afraid of my granddaddy's outhouse. I thought there was a monster who lived in the cess-pit. Every time I went out to take a crap, I was sure it was going to reach up and grab my b . . ."

"Walt!"

"It's okay, Uncle Walt, I have three brothers. I know about that stuff." Had Janie been in a better mood, she might have giggled.

Walter was clearly embarrassed. He cleared his throat. "Any-way, like I was saying, I went back last summer to visit and the darn place still gives me the creeps!"

"That's 5—'cept'n 5 is a real monster who lives in my head. It followed me here, and it won't leave me alone!" Janie said in a very small voice, "5 is going to do something . . . something bad . . . Maybe even hurt somebody and I can't control it!"

"Whew! That's some story, kid. Is that all you're worried about! I must say it comes as a bit of a relief. Here I thought you was going to tell us you was some kind of escaped des-perado, one of Dillinger's gun molls on the lam, or worse, a pint-size Nazi spy!"

It was no use. Uncle Walt didn't believe a word of it—no-body did. Janie sighed and reluctantly climbed on the make-up chair. She laid a towel around her neck. "Uncle Walt, you can put my make-up on now."

Chapter 11

Christmas in July

Providence, Rhode Island, the last stand before Hartford, and the big show was throwing itself a party. One of Ringling Bros. Circus' long-standing traditions: Christmas on the fourth of July. Never in her whole life had Janie ever heard of anything quite so silly, or nearly so much fun! The cookhouse was gaily decorated with American flags, tinsel, and red and green crepe paper streamers. The kitchen staff was busy preparing heaping platters of fried chicken, ham, mashed potatoes, and peas. Janie hated peas! This was the one day out of the year when everyone was allowed to sit anywhere, roustabouts, management, performers alike. Everyone seemed in high spirits, and Janie especially was enjoying a grand time! She sat with her friend, Aarti, and his father. They were Hindu and didn't celebrate Christmas, but they seemed to be enjoying the cake and ice cream just the same.

"Gimme a buzz, angelface!"

Some well-meaning fool made the mistake of hanging up mistletoe, and Janie unintentionally blundered underneath. Sparkles took advantage of every opportunity. Against her better judgment, she gave in and allowed the obnoxious dwarf a quick peck on the cheek. Never one to pass up the chance to kiss the girls, the lecherous dwarf planted one on her, full on the mouth. Yuck!

"Merry Christmas, Uncle Walt!" Janie kissed Walt. "I love you."

"You're pretty terrific yourself, kid." This time Janie didn't even mind when he called her "the kid."

Bobby Segee watched as the stupid puppet-girl laughed, chirped, and sang Christmas carols. His hate boiled over; he would break those bones. He took out the worn box of matches and turned it over in his hand. He couldn't read very well, but he knew the words written on the box: *Compliments of the Alleo Motel.* There were just two matches left. His special matches, the ones the "Red Man" gave him. The ones he used to set fires.

"Go and laugh, Janie McConaughey, 'cause tonight your world ends in fire."

* * *

On the way back, Walter and Janie took the long way around past the circus train siding. "One of the first things you got to learn if you're going to hang 'round the circus kid, is what you see here—all 78 cars is a whole city on wheels. We never stay in one place more than a couple of days. It takes a heap 'o folks to put on a show the size of Big Bertha, 'least that's what the competition calls us."

"Golly, how many people?" Janie was amazed.

"Oh, 'round twelve hundred, I reckon. That's down from before the war, not count'n the electricians, carpenters, and roustabouts. You got your stake teams on the flying squadron; they lay out the lot. Cageboys mostly feed the stock 'n clean the stalls and the bullmen, they handle the elephants. I grew up on a ranch in Texas, so I know my way around horses. This here is your baggage stock. These are the horses we use for work. Then there's ring stock, they're the performing horses. It's a good way to earn cherry pie."

Janie crinkled her nose, "That's goofy, how come they give you a cherry pie for help'n out with the horses?"

"Cherry pie, that's circus-talk for extra pay for extra work."

"That's real neat, Uncle Walt, and here I thought the circus was just a bunch of clowns, lion tamers, and a guy on a flying trapeze." Janie favored her friend with a dimpled grin.

Not everything about life on the road was exciting. Some of it was pretty gosh darn ordinary. There were beds to be made, floors to be swept, and dishes to be done. Walt did most of the cooking. "Get up, kid, time for breakfast."

"So early?" Janie whined. She felt irritable and cross and more than a little anxious as to her chance meeting with Bobby Segee, "Not if we're going to eat at Hotel Dukie . . . 'Cos if we are, I'll just sleep in." She tossed the blanket over her head and pretended to snore loudly.

"Oh no, you don't!" Walt whipped back the covers. Janie squealed. "Com'on, up with the chickens! I'm going to make you pancakes super-duper-deluxe—a venerable recipe entrusted to me by a maharajah, one of the great kings of Timbuktu, or was it a greasy-spoon fry cook in Cincinnati? I can't remember which."

The promise of pancakes was enough to coax the sleepy eleven-year-old off the top bunk. Pancakes were her favorite and Mother never made pancakes except on Sunday.

"These sure are good pancakes!"

Pancakes was one of Walter's specialties, but the bachelor clown was kind of a slob, and Janie soon discovered he could dirty a whole sink full of dishes just making a cup of tea! After she made the beds, swept the trailer, doing the dishes was her job, and that meant fetching water. Ordinarily, she didn't mind, as there was always something interesting to see on the walk over to the water truck. A circus ground is a busy place, and Janie enjoyed her morning conversations with "Swift" the loin steak pail. Not this morning—the girl was just about as nervous as a long-tailed cat in-a-room-full-of-rocking-chairs.

"What's bothering you, kid, you ain't said two words all morning?" Swift creaked.

"I got troubles . . . I seen this boy yesterday," Janie said, while keeping a sharp eye out for big dumb Bobby Segee.

"Well, why you didn't say somth'n in the first place? Romance is my specialty!" The pail squeaked, "I was smitten with a faucet once, Flo was her name . . ."

"No, you don't understand. This boy hates me!"

"Not to worry, acrimonious break-ups just happens to be my other specialty. Take Jack and Jill, for example, it's a common misconception that they were together. Not true, Jill hated Jack. That whole up-the-hill-to-fetch-a-pail-of-water, nothing but dodge so Jill could push poor Jack down the hill! And the tumbling after—forget about it, a complete cover-up!"

"Oh, you're no help—I'm wasting my time talking to an upidstay pail."

"Henry and Liza, now there's another pair of star-crossed lovers . . ."

"Aw, shut up!"

* * *

The clown spec was in full swing. Janie was in the kitchen. The eggs plunked into the bowl. She churned the egg-beater vigorously, spattering the cardboard set with cake batter. This is where Walter, the consummate showman, added something he called a "stop." Janie yucked it up for the crowd and paused to light a cigar. The sheer inappropriateness of the gag alone—of an obvious child smoking a cigar, elicited huge guffaws from the crowd. Janie was a natural comic. The puppet-girl put the cake in the oven. Boom! The girl reappeared, her frizzy hair slightly smoking, the cigar burst like a banana peel—and her face black as a minstrel player.

The crowd howled with laughter.

"Hello, fire department, I want to report a fire."

Segee's hellish plan called to wait until the big top filled to capacity. When the clown spec was in full swing, when the stupid puppet-girl came out and told her stupid joke. He struck a match and set light to the north sidewall by the blue grandstand.

"Where's the fire, miss?" Bill Ding Jr. answered on the other line.

"It's in the kitchen."

Bobby didn't get the joke. He never understood why the stupid girl didn't simply tell the fire department her address? The audience laughed every time—they were twice as stupid! They wouldn't be laughing for long.

"How do we get there?"

"You got a truck, don't you?"

The fire started on the curtain wall, no larger than a pinhole. Even untreated, the canvas was a tinderbox ready to burn. Bobby had phantasms of mass hysteria, animals braying, people screaming, trampling, the specter of the big top engulfed, burning, burning like a wick of a Roman candle.

An alert seatman on duty doused the flames with a five-gallon bucket. Bobby Segee grimaced; he cursed his foul luck. He had one match left. He made up his mind to try again in Hartford—this time behind the men's toilets where no one could see until it was too late.

* * *

"What do you mean, you can't get the gas? I need two hundred gallons of gasoline on the Barbour Street lot by nine a.m. Thursday. Do what you have to." Leonard Aylesworth was on the phone to his twenty-four-hour man in Hartford. With the war rationing, it seemed his man was having trouble securing the fuel the circus needed to operate, never mind getting it delivered on the fourth of July. The superintendent crushed out his cigarette and looked up at the seatman. "Two fires in two shows, huh? Probably just some kids burning a hole with a cigarette, trying to steal a peek without paying! I wouldn't worry about it." Aylesworth never gave the fire a second thought, he'd had bigger headaches. "I don't care—steal the damn stuff if you have to. Tell 'em no gas—no show, do you understand?"

* * *

Sidney cried for days.

For a whole week, they searched. They searched the swamp, dragged the river. State police tracking dogs picked up her trail and followed as far as a gravel verge of the no. 49 cutoff of the Penn Central main track. There was no sign, no trace, the girl had simply vanished.

"Whoa!" Mr. Sponzo pulled on the reins and climbed down off his mowing machine. The work was hot and dusty, the grass was dry, and it hadn't rained for days. The twenty-four-hour man contracted him to mow and rake the Barbour Street grounds. It was a long rectangular lot. For most of the year, it stood vacant, an empty grassy field. Some of the neighborhood children used it as a ball field and Sponzo could vaguely see the dusty outline of the batter's box and the trampled ruts between the bases.

Now something was fouling his mower blades. All morning long he'd had trouble with bits of wire and tin cans catching and clattering in the clockworks. As Sponzo worked to clear the debris between the tines, something caught his eye, something that was not a bit of wire. It was a scrap of paper with a child's face.

MISSING GIRL
Jane Elizabeth McConaughey: Age 11, 4'2", 69 lbs.
Blue-green eyes, blonde hair, last seen wearing a green
sweater and white pinafore dress. Contact Hartford County
Sheriff's department or the Connecticut State Police.

Chapter 12

The Prodigal Child

The circus train was late. It seemed ever since the big show left Sarasota on the first of May, they had been late for every engagement for one reason or another. The jump from Providence to Hartford was a short 90 miles; nevertheless, they were five hours late pulling into the Windsor Street siding. This was wartime America and civilian rail freight was strictly rationed. The Ringling Bros. Circus was the rare exception, granted special rail privileges by the government; its entertainment value was deemed a necessity to wartime morale.

Mr. Healy blamed the railroads, and the railroads blamed the flatcars the circus used to transport the poles for the top. The big top was new that year. The largest tent in the world and the extra-long cars were unable to negotiate the sharp curves, and the circus train was rerouted.

Blowing a show was bad luck, very bad luck. Circus folks were superstitious by nature, and it didn't help any that their lives were fraught with dangerous circumstances beyond their control. Fire was a constant danger, aerialists could fall from their apparatus, and animals were forever unpredictable.

Whistling was considered an especially inveterate crotchet, a superstition of which Janie ran afoul when she innocently whistled in the dressing tent. Sparkles blew a gasket, and the clown sent the girl packing. He made her face north, stand on one foot and turn around three times before allowing her back in.

Ever since the fatal fall of the great aerialist, Lillian Leitzel, in '31, Merle Evans, the bandleader, refused to play *"Crimson Petal,"* her music playing at the time of the accident. It was considered bad luck to look back while participating in a circus parade, as were peanuts on the floor. However, blowing a show, that was the worst!

The stake teams were hard at work; the cookhouse went up, as did the sideshow and dressing room tents. Not even the prolific, caustic cursing of Whitey Versteeg or the superhuman effort of the roustabouts could make up for lost time. It was almost noon, too late to set up for the two o'clock matinee. The show was blown.

* * *

"Do I hafta, Uncle Walt? I don't see why I have to go home now just because we're in dumb ol' Hartford."

"Don't you miss your mom and dad?"

"Not really, they don't care about me, anyway."

"You and I both know that's not true!"

"What about your friends?"

"I don't have any friends . . . You guys are my friends! I want to stay here with you and Em!"

"I'm not going to argue with you anymore. You're too young to understand, but there're laws in this country. A little thing called kidnapping. People tend to frown on that sort of thing. Em's right, we should have put you on a bus a week ago. I got to protect myself." "Let me do the show one more time. Please."

"You're going home, kid, show's over!"

Janie scrunched down in the front seat of the borrowed Studebaker and sulked.

The house on Elm Street looked serene, well-kept, neat, trim, and tidy. Certainly not the sort of house Walt expected to find. Suspiciously, there was not a single sign that any children lived here, not a bat, a ball, bicycle, or wagon. No evidence at all to indicate this was the home of four active children.

"Are you sure this is where you live, kid?"

"Sure, Uncle Walt. 625 Elm Street, that's where I live all right."

"Then I guess this is good-bye."

"Aren't you coming in?"

"Nah, I'd just get in the way, see you around, kid." Walt awkwardly offered to shake Janie's hand, but the girl would have none of it.

"I love you, Uncle Walt." Janie hugged the clown and kissed him on the cheek. "Uncle Walt, you're crying."

"Just something in my eye, kid, that's all. Go on, Janie, get oughta here." (That was the first and the only time Walter ever called her Janie). "Here's twenty dollars, you earned it. You know we would have put you on a bus sooner . . ."

"Don't worry, Uncle Walt. I won't get you into any trouble. I'll tell 'em that I wouldn't tell you my last name or where I lived or nothing, so you couldn't send me home."

Walter smiled, "That's my girl."

Janie rang the doorbell. A severe Frau Detweiler answered the door. The housekeeper peered down at the little girl as if she were a grease spot on her impeccably clean kitchen floor.

"Who is it, Frau?" Mr. Paradise called from his study.

"It is ze jung fräulein Herr Paradise, ze one who is missing, ze one who causes so much trouble."

"Janie!" Jim ran to the door.

"Mr. Paradise! Mr. Paradise, I'm home, I've come back! I've had so many adventures and real ones this time!" Janie was earnest, and for the first time, she was actually glad to be home.

"Mein gott, fräulein, where have you been? We've been worried sick about you. We thought you were kidnapped, or worse!"

"Aren't you glad to see me, Mr. Paradise?"

"You've been a very naughty little girl."

"Und very dirty little girl from ze looks of things," Frau Detweiler added disapprovingly.

Although Em and Walter had done their best, the two clowns lacked the experience, the fineness, required for the care and upkeep of an eleven-year-old girl. The child before them was tousled, rumpled, and grubby. Her hair was tangled, and her face still smeared with telltale traces of clown white. Her once beautiful white pinafore was ripped and tattered. Even though Abe the Monday Man had done his best to wash and mend it, Janie's dress was a couple of shades this side of gray.

"Come in the house, fräulein, you must be starving. Frau, see if there is anything in the icebox, some milk, and a slice of that braunschweiger we had at lunch."

"Is there any strudel, Mrs. Detweiler? I sure do like your strudel."

At the mention of her famous strudel, Frau Detweiler's face betrayed a thin Mona Lisa smile before her composure returned to her usual stern demeanor.

"I'll telephone the Sheriff at once."

"Oh please, Mr. Paradise, don't do that! You mustn't tell anyone I'm here. Please, can't I just stay with you a couple of days?"

"Absolutely not! I don't have any choice in the matter, Frau, get the Sheriff on the line."

"No! Just take me home. Please, Mr. Paradise, don't call the Sheriff, he hates me!"

"Does he now? Okay, we take you home. I'll get the truck."

"Not like that. She looks like und hobo!" Frau Detweiler objected.

"She is very dirty. Telling me fräulein, where have you been all this time?"

"Oh, I've been lots of places. I ran away and joined the circus! I got to be a clown. I jumped out of a burning building, and I saw lions and got to ride an elephant and . . ." Janie was breathless. The story was all true, but in the telling, it sounded so fantastic she paused to wonder if any of it really happened. She fretted silently, what if none of it happened? What if it all had been just one big phantasmagoria—one of her horrible hallucinations? She could never be sure.

"Are these more of your lies?"

"No, sir, honest, I was a clown in the circus. I learned how to juggle and I told my joke in front of six-thousand people."

A pained expression crossed Jim's face. He loved the child dearly, but she troubled him the way she was always telling lies. "Please Janie, no more lies."

"I can so juggle!" The girl picked up three apples from the fruit bowl.

Jim was amused. Even if she was lying, the child was a wonder. Now where did she learn to do that? "Frau, be so kind take our little Janie upstairs and see that she has a bath, fix her hair and let me see those shoes."

Jim frowned at the deplorable condition of the girl's shoes. He took out the brush and bootblack from his shoeshine kit and began to buff the girl's shoes. He'd always liked shining shoes. He found the activity satisfying. He hummed softly a little song his father used to sing when he was a boy.

> ♫ *Cobbler, cobbler, mend my shoe.*
> *Give it one stitch, give it two.*
> *Give it three, give it four.*
> *And if it needs it, give it more.* ♫

> *Telling me my little Firefly, where have your*

shoes been? I wonder.

Jim Paradise glanced at an advertisement in the *Hartford Courant:* Annual Fourth of July Sale, G. Fox's department store. Frau was right; he couldn't take the little prodigal child home, not looking like a ragamuffin. Jim had an idea. He hollered up the stairs, "Then we'll all take a drive downtown, and Frau, don't forget my ration coupon book."

Chapter 13

The Dilly Girl

"I don't know, twenty-two dollars!" Jim Paradise fingered the price tag. He stood nervously, awkwardly, in the young misses department at G. Fox's department store. Three dresses later, and he felt less like he was buying a pair of work boots and more like he was playing with paper dolls.

Janie put on a pout.

"Oh, Janie, I didn't mean it like that, I love it. The dress—I think you're beautiful! What do you think, Frau?"

"Ja, Herr Paradise, ze jung mädchen is very attraktiv."

"There still seems to be something missing, she needs . . .ah, something more." Jim gestured helplessly. Frau Detweiler came to the rescue. She knew exactly what was missing, the one article of clothing every young girl requires, aspiring to feel feminine.

"Ach, und *büstenhalter!*"

The attentive clerk at G. Fox whisked Janie off to the fitting room. When she emerged, she felt very shy but very grown-up. Janie did indeed look pretty; her bright face beamed. Never in her whole life had she had so many adults give her such attention. She pirouetted, twirled, and struck a pose like Betty Grable.

Jim didn't know quite what to say. He managed a weak, "mein fräulein." Jim smiled, nodded, and added under his breath . . . *Ach, that was what was missing.*

* * *

"Wait in the truck," Jim said in a voice that made clear he was used to giving orders.

Jim Paradise knocked on the door of the McConaughey home; this was going to be awkward, he thought. A distraught, but composed Mrs. McConaughey answered the door.

"Good afternoon Mrs. McConaughey, my name is Jim Paradise. We haven't met, but I have some information regarding your daughter."

"About Janie? Are you from the FBI? Bob! There's a man here who says he knows something about Janie!"

"Jim Paradise."

"Come in, Mr. Paradise. Have they found her?"

Paula began to cry, "Oh please dear god—tell me she isn't dead!"

"She's alive, Mrs. McConaughey, we found her, or rather Janie found me. She's outside in the truck right now."

"Janie!"

"She's afraid, Mr. McConaughey, apparently afraid of you. She thinks you'll spank her, or shut her in her room."

"I'll do no such thing!"

"I want to believe you, Mr. McConaughey. Janie seems to think otherwise."

"My daughter has a wild imagination."

"She does stretch the truth a bit sometimes."

"Are you some kind of law officer?"

"No, just a friend of Janie."

"Then you have no say in the matter. Get out of my way!"

"As you wish, your daughter is in the truck."

Janie Firefly, fugitive felon and public enemy no. 1 surrendered to the authorities at four o'clock. She stepped out of the Model A Ford pickup, greeted by the pop and flash of Speed Graflex and a battery of reporters' questions.

"Miss Firefly, Avery Kirk, *Hartford Courant.* How do you respond to the accusation that you broke your bedroom window?"

"No comment."

There was a second flurry of flashbulbs.

"Miss Firefly, are you aware federal prosecutors filed papers in the district court placing a five-dollar lien against your allowance?"

Janie smiled and waved to the crowd; she looked very pretty in her new blue-checked dress and fresh blue hair ribbons. Her shoes were polished; even her knee socks were crisp and white. She had two tickets for the circus and a twenty-dollar bill. She didn't run, she walked to the front door with a deliberate, defiant cadence. If her parents were expecting her to be sorry, they were in for a powerful disappointment. She wasn't sorry, not in the least! She'd do it again in a minute. So many adventures, real adventures, not any made-up, make-believe adventures. It had all been worth it.

"Hello, Daddy, I'm home."

"Good-bye, Mr. Paradise." Robert showed Jim the door.

Janie watched as her friend, her hero, Mr. Paradise, left. She stood very small and quiet, waiting for the screaming and hollering to begin. There was dead silence throughout the room. Robert was very explicit to his wife regarding the conditions of their daughter's return. He warned Paula sternly, when Janie came home, not to make a scene. There was to be no fussing, no joyous homecoming, no reward. Janie was to march straight to her room.

"Paula, don't!"

Paula didn't care. Janie was her only daughter, and she was home, safe and alive! She could hold back no longer. She ran and threw her arms around her, hugged her, and smothered her in kisses, sobbing and laughing all at once. "Oh, sweetheart, I love you so much. We were so worried about you!"

"Janie, go to your room."

Janie was never so disrespectful as to act snooty, smarty, or snotty in front of her parents. She knew better. They deserved better—but she sure felt like it inside. Janie passed Sidney lurking in the kitchen. "Hello, Sid, did you miss me?"

* * *

Janie crept into her father's study and closed the pocket doors. They said she couldn't leave the house, and this wasn't exactly leaving the house, and she was quite sure nobody said anything about not using the telephone. She picked up the telephone and dialed.

"Hello, fire department, I want to report a fire."

"Where's the fire, miss?"

"It's in the kitchen."

"How do we get there?"

"You've got a truck, don't you?" Janie snickered and almost fudged her whole plan.

"Is this some kind of joke, kid?"

"Oh no sir, I'm just scared . . . I'm home alone. My mommy and daddy are at work, and my big brother went to the store. He told me not to touch the stove!"

"Calm down, now do you know your address?"

"Yes sir, my address is D-211 Stuart Avenue, and please hurry!" The fire chief said something about getting out of the house as fast as possible. Janie cracked a sly grin. That was exactly what she planned to do.

Janie closed her eyes and counted to one-hundred. She picked up the receiver and called the cab company. She asked the driver to pick her up two blocks over on Staples Street. It was a good plan, a gosh darn clever plan. She checked to make sure the two tickets were still in her pocket. The twenty-dollar bill was pinned inside her slip. She waited until she heard the wail of the siren and headed for the back door. In the ensuing chaos, it was a simple matter for one very small, naughty little girl to slip out the back door unnoticed, jump the hedge, and cut across Mrs. Sheppard's yard over to Staples Street. What could possibly go wrong?

"Where the heck do you think you're going? Did you call the fire department? I'm gonna tell Mom!"

"Fuck!" It was Sid the rat! And she didn't mean crud, fud, or fiddlesticks, either.

"Fuck, fuck, fuck!"

"Mom! Janie is cursing again!"

"Shut up, Sid!"

"Why should I? I'm gonna tell Mom and you'll be in even more trouble!"

"Sidney, if you don't tell—I'll take you with me." Janie couldn't believe what she just said, and she was immediately sorry for her offer.

"Where are we going?"

"To the circus, now hurry up."

"Jeepers!"

Janie grabbed her brother by the hand and practically took him hostage; she dragged him off the back porch and over the hedge. The two children cut through Mrs. Sheppard's back-yard, ducked under her clean laundry flapping on the line, and ran as fast as they could to Staples Street.

It was just four blocks over to Vine Street, Charlie's house. She paid the cab driver with the twenty-dollar bill and told him to wait.

"You can't sit with us, and I don't want you hanging around. Here's two dollars, that's enough money for grandstand seats and all the soda and popcorn you can eat!"

"This is Charlie's house, is he your boyfriend? Are you going on a date? That's weird 'cos Charlie doesn't like girls."

"He likes me."

"Are you gonna kiss him?"

"Shut up, Sid." . . . *I just might,* Janie thought.

* * *

Janie was too naïve to know it—but her best friend Charlie had a cob crosswise, provoked, jealous, more likely. His entire life he'd wanted more than anything to break into show business, and here his best friend went and fell "back-asswards" into the circus without even trying! The girl performed in front of thousands of cheering people in The Greatest Show on Earth, and the worst part was she used his jokes! Janie remained completely innocent as to her blunder. Charlie reminded himself that she was loyal, sincere; the girl meant no harm. Besides, she was such a happy and agreeable companion, Charlie found it difficult to stay angry with her for very long.

There was so much excitement, so many things to see and do. There was Baby Thelma the fat lady, Rasmus Neilsen the strongman, and Hanka Kelter the bearded lady. There was the usual collection of freaks, sword swallowers, and tattooed ladies. Charlie liked the guy who pounded nails up his nose, The Human Blockhead.

"Now there's an act!"

It was all such colossal fun! Janie had sixteen dollars and forty-seven cents left, enough money to see ten circuses, so they saw everything, twice. Janie and Charlie feasted on cotton candy, caramel apples, hot dogs, and pink lemonade. They rode the carousel, thrilled on the whirligig, and laughed themselves silly in the funhouse.

Janie clasped Charlie by the hand and together the two children raced up and down the midway. She wanted to show Charlie everything. Janie was something of a minor celebrity. Everywhere she went, barkers, talkers, and even the working-acts greeted her by name. "Hello, Janie Firefly!"

It was getting on 'till two o'clock, almost show time and there was still Gargantua, the world's most terrifying living creature. Or so Janie thought, that was until she ran smack dab into Crissy Greene with her new boyfriend, Ronnie-Ray.

"Well, lookee see who's gammin', if it isn't crazy Janie Mc-Conaughey all dolled up and her four-eyed creepy boyfriend! Well, ain't you just a dilly girl!"

Oh no, it was Crissy Greene all right, and to make matters worse, *and what could be worse?* She was wearing the exact same lace-trimmed sateen blouse, and twirly blue-and-white checked dress, right down to the same pretty cerulean hair ribbons, the dress Mr. Paradise not only paid $22 for, but also used twenty-eight ration coupons. What were the chances of that? Janie was mortified. This was worse than a disaster. It was a catastrophe! Suddenly, Janie felt a whole lot less togged-to-the-bricks and more like a country hurkle. Crissy sized up Janie as if she were an insect in need of squashing. She turned up a snooty nose and strutted past.

"Com'on, Ronnie, you promised to buy me some cotton candy."

"Atwhay away upidstay itchbay." Charlie squeezed Janie's hand, "Com'on, Janie. We still got five tickets left, let's go ride the whirligig!" With that one squeeze, Charlie affirmed Janie's self-esteem. She smiled; her dimpled grin told the whole story. Crissy was one of those fast broads who'd been around the block. Crissy took boys out behind the shed. Oh sure, her hair was more luxurious, and she had way bigger you-know-whats. The two girls may have been wearing the same dress, but the way Janie figured it—she had Crissy Greene beat-all-to-heck in the brains, smile, and personality department.

It was showtime, and Janie was eager to see her friends. She'd never actually seen the circus from the grandstand. The energy of the crowd was electric. She clapped and cheered and bounced in her seat. She was so excited.

"Isn't this great, Chucky!"

Charlie was excited too, in his own quiet, reserved way. These were great seats; Walter had personally seen to it that the kids had some of the best in the house. Janie slurped down her third Coke. She squirmed in her seat. The big cat act with May Kovar was coming to a finale. She couldn't concentrate on big cats, or anything else, for that matter. All she could think about was the three Cokes she'd drunk on the midway. Suddenly, she was beginning to regret her excess.

Janie whispered to Charlie, "Chucky, I have to go to the bathroom."

"Hurry up, upidstay, the Wallendas are about to perform." Charlie looked to the high-wire. The beam of the klieg spotlight circled, coalesced, and finally sought out Karl Wallenda, forty feet above the circus floor. There was no net. Janie hurried.

* * *

Bobby Segee lurked beside the entrance to the men's toilets. He watched as she entered the big top, all gay and happy in her fancy blue-checked dress with her queer, four-eyed boyfriend. Oh, how he hated that girl! His volcanic vengeance welled up inside him; a seething cauldron of caustic enmity lay black and twisted in his bowels. He fingered the match, his last one. He was sweating profusely, his jaw clenched; the match flared and sputtered to life.

He watched the stupid girl laugh and chirp; she drank a third Coke. It was only a matter of time.

Janie lost her way—on her way back to her seat—the fifth-grader got turned around somehow and almost blundered into the men's washroom.

Segee grabbed the girl by the throat and pushed her hard against the canvas sidewall. The girl struggled, choked, and kicked; her feet dangled. He pressed his hand against her mouth so she couldn't scream. Ten minutes into the live animal act, the crowd was transfixed. Merle Evans and the band played a spirited march. It wasn't as if there was anyone who could have heard.

In the trash can behind the men's washroom, the fire burned.

"I ain't a feard of you, 'n I ain't a feard of yer weirdo made-up friends neither! I've kilt three little girls, same as you. You had this coming fer a long time!" The ribbons in her hair were the same, the same frilly blue-and-white-checked dress. Bobby Segee took his hand away from her mouth, on account he liked to kiss the girls before he killed them. Smoke filled the confined space. There was very little time.

Segee held the girl by the throat, high up against the curtain wall; her feet thrashed, kicked, and finally fell silent. The girl was already dead.

Janie looked behind her. On the sidewall was a circle of flame. She blinked, squinted. There, silhouetted, perfectly backlit against the canvas, was a man holding a girl by her throat. The girl kicked and struggled. The whole scene played out as if some macabre shadow play staged by Henri Rivière.

"Oh, gawd, not again!" Janie's mind had been clear for so many days, now it was happening all over again. The circle of flames was still quite small. At first, she thought it was part of the show.

It was not part of the show.

Chapter 14

One Minute

The arena went dark; the music stopped. A hushed silence fell over the audience as a single spotlight illuminated a man standing alone four stories above the arena floor. Eight thousand people collectively looked up and simultaneously gasped. Karl Wallenda raised his hand and tested the tension with one foot. The oppressive July heat was greatest near the peak, and the wire was temperature-sensitive. Satisfied, he stepped out onto the wire. Merle Evans and the band began the first bars of a quiet waltz.

Weary Willie entered the ring, the only other act allowed to perform while the Wallendas walked the wire. The sad face tramp shuffled around the track in his floppy shoes and hobo clothes as he tried repeatedly, without success, to sweep away the beam of a spotlight with his tattered broom.

High overhead, the Flying Wallendas, the greatest circus act in the world, assembled. They wore beautiful yellow costumes, all feathers and sequins. They carried chairs on their shoulders and were about to walk a wire that stretched the length of all three rings, without a net.

The curious girl blundered around the corner. The simple mistake of turning left instead of right was about to cost Janie her life. Bobby Segee saw her first. When she saw him—when she saw what was happening—she let out a yelp, unprepared for the gruesome confrontation. Segee held the lifeless girl by the throat. The half-witted boy was baffled. His poor retarded brain wracked; his frustrations mounted as he tried desperately to reconcile the reality of the situation. The dead girl crumpled to the ground, demoted, rejected, like a wallflower prom date nobody wanted to dance with anyway. Bobby gave chase after the live girl in the blue-checked dress.

Janie ran.

"You'll get yours, you stupid little bitch!"

"Help me, 5!"

Segee was bigger and stronger, and Janie didn't have much of a head start. There was no way for the eleven-year-old to escape, not this time.

"I don't think so." A wicked grin traversed the mischievous imp's jaw. Oh, how it hated that girl. 5 hated her with every fiber of its immoral being; it enjoyed reaping misfortune and misery on its mistress at every opportunity. The boy, however, was an interloper, a pretender, a usurper, and that irked 5—the girl belonged only to it—and nobody was going to bedevil the girl but 5!

5 stuck out a slithery claw. The act of Janie's salvation was purely evil and self-serving; this was unfinished business. 5 seemed to remember harboring an especially corrupt hatred for the big dumb boy. Besides, the devilish homunculus didn't mind a bit heaping out a dose of freelance mischief. The thing shrieked with laughter when the clumsy boy tripped and fell face-first into the sawdust.

Already the flames were licking the leading edge of the roof.

Segee tripped over a guy cable and fell flat on his face. The beast that was fire—his own progeny, raced up the laces used to connect the sidewalls, the hemp material burned like dry kindling, popping and snapping. The fire licked, always seeking more fuel. A flaming scrap of canvas tore loose and fell burning on the boy's back. This time, it was Segee's turn to scream. He'd had enough. He knew better than anyone the holocaust that was about to ensue once the fire reached the roof. The craven coward licked his wounds and fled the tent. Janie never saw him again—not that she ever looked back.

* * *

"Aren't you afraid of anything, Uncle Walt?"
"Just fire, kid, fire is the all-time nightmare
in the circus business."
"Jeepers, how would I ever know? I mean, if there was a fire?"
"Oh, we circus folks have our ways. Listen kid,
if you ever hear Mr. Evans play Starts and Stripes Forever,
that's the disaster march for circus people.
I want you to run as fast as you can out of the top,
promise me that?"
"That's easy, Uncle Walt, if I hear Stars and Stripes Forever,
that means fire."

* * *

The girl ran in a blind state of terror. Segee had frightened her enough—but the specter of fire frightened her more. She ducked back through the tunnel into the top and slammed headlong into the arms of usher Mike Dare.

"Ticket, miss?"

The head usher cut off her path.

"Whoa, slow down, kid, you're gonna hurt someone tearing around like that."

"I don't have a ticket." Janie's hand went to her pocket. If she'd ever had a ticket, the terrified girl was never going to find it.

"Please, sir, I've got to get back in the tent. My brother is in there!"

Charlie was in there, too. Janie, in her heightened state of panic, forgot all about her best friend. It was all her fault; her own selfishness brought her brother to the circus. Her little brother was a rat and a pest; he was only nine years old and dumb as a bag of hammers, but he was her responsibility. If anything happened to Sidney, her mother and father would never forgive her! Aw heck, she'd never forgive herself. In the consternation of the moment, Janie had a trice of clarity. She realized something about herself. She loved her brother.

"Sorry, miss, I can't let you back in without your ticket stub."

The usher wasn't listening.

"Lemme go!" Janie jerked away. "There's fire in the men's bathroom!"

The words "fire" had the desired effect. Janie dove between the man's legs and wriggled out the other side. Dare summoned the three ushers in his section. The men cut behind the southwest blues and grabbed the fire buckets. There were four buckets, each filled with four gallons of water. All four buckets were thrown on the flames, without effect. In a desperate attempt to prevent the fire from reaching the roof, Dare and his ushers tried to pull down the sidewall. By this time, the fire was out of control, an indefatigable beast.

Charlie looked around, behind, and in the direction Janie left to go to the bathroom. Janie had been gone a long time, and Charlie was getting worried. If the upidstay girl didn't hurry, she was going to miss the Wallendas. There was some commotion coming from the aisles behind him. Charlie turned to look towards the disturbance, as did most people in the section sitting next to him. Charlie knew Janie well, or at least he thought he did. The girl was capable of some wild, crazy things, but what happened next topped any crazy stunt the girl had ever done. Charlie was flabbergasted to see Janie Firefly running full tilt down the aisle, with two irate ushers in pursuit.

"Stop that girl!"

"Janie!" Charlie tried to get Janie's attention. Janie didn't hear Charlie. She hopped the low iron railing and ran across the arena, through the gap between the steel ring cage, and dashed across the hippodrome track to a smattering of applause. The crowd thought it was part of the show. It was not part of the show. Janie ran past Emmett Kelly, across the third ring, and over to the bandstand. She landed ass-over-tea-kettle in a heap at the foot of one very perturbed Merle Evans.

The band missed a beat.

Janie looked up; her eyes were wild and full of fear. "Mr. Evans, f-fire! Mr. Evans, there's fire in the big top!"

High on the wire, Karl saw the fire. One of their bikes fell to the sawdust below. It was too late. The flames had already reached the roof.

Chapter 15

Stars and Stripes Forever

The afternoon of July 6, 1944, was sunny, hot, and humid. World War II was in its fifth year, one month after D-Day. Despite the gasoline rationing, thousands of fans made their way to the Barbour Street grounds in Hartford, Connecticut, to see the Ringling Bros. and Barnum & Bailey Circus.

The day was a scorcher, a blazing eighty-eight degrees, and the crowd was dressed for the weather. Boys were in shorts, girls in sunsuits, and men loosened their ties and carried their jackets draped over their arms. A day at the circus was a joyous, carefree occasion all of Hartford looked forward to with nearly the same ardent anticipation as Christmas.

Evans' baton wavered, hovered, and paused in mid-beat. He looked down sternly at one very small, frightened little girl in a heap at the foot of his podium. It was the precocious "Firefly" girl, the puppet-girl from the burning house spec who told the silly "fire-in-the-kitchen" joke. The maestro was prepared to be very cross with the child.

"If this is your idea of a joke, young lady . . ." One look at the stark terror etched on the young girl's face revealed to the conductor this horror was no joke.

"Fire, Mr. Evans!" Oh, how Janie wished it was a lie. *Please dear God, make it a lie.* Of all the millions of horrible lies she'd ever told, why couldn't this be one of them? Janie scrunched up her face and wished with all her might, "Please be a lie." The pop and snap of the flames told the truth.

Evans saw the fire. He shouted to Branda, the ringmaster, who was already running towards the bandstand with the original intent of corralling one very small, naughty little girl. The girl had created a disturbance, interrupted the show, and Branda was not happy.

The coruscate flames wavered ever higher up the side of the cavernous tent, devouring canvas, sisal, and paraffin. What was once a little fire suddenly shot upwards with nightmarish speed and billowed across the roof of the top. Branda saw the smoke and blew a shrill blast on his whistle to halt the Wallendas and raced out the performers' exit to warn the next acts.

One minute passed.

Evans' baton rose. The twenty-nine-piece band, in their white and gold uniforms, were to their feet. "Blast it, boys!" Without regard to his own safety, the bandsman and the orchestra brass struck up John Philip Sousa's *"Stars and Stripes Forever."* All over the Barbour Street lot, the roustabouts, roughnecks, and the circus workers knew something terrible was happening in the main tent.

In clown alley, Walter was preparing for his walkaround. He was putting the finishing touches on his garish make-up when he heard the alarm, *Stars and Stripes*—he glanced out the flap. Already, the tent was burning with a celluloid fierceness. In that terrible moment, Walter felt as though someone punched him in the gut. He'd given the girl two tickets for the matinee.

Janie was in the big top! Tears ran in rivulets, tracing clean streaks on his clown-white face.

Janie heard ringmaster Fred Branda urge the audience to remain calm and to leave in an orderly fashion, but the power failed, and he could not be heard. A few alert people, halting, began to make their way to the exits. The crowd was packed, cheek by jowl; their movements were glacial and hesitant. The fans in the grandstands remained transfixed. Most people thought it was somehow part of the show. It was not part of the show. An usher in the front row saw the blaze—as did a man returning to his seat with a Coke. The man pointed with the bottle and yelled, "fire!"

A girl in the bleachers felt the heat behind her, and turned to ask her mother, "Mommy, is the tent supposed to be on fire?"

Some people did turn to look, but most were captivated by the spotlight. They didn't want to miss one second of the Wallendas' spellbinding act. The crowd came to the circus that day to be entertained. Their minds were caught up with happy expectations, and they couldn't easily switch from a mood of frivolity and anticipation to the reality of the catastrophe about to befall them. Others assumed that some circus employee would certainly arrive to put out the fire, and the day's amusement wouldn't be spoiled. Tongues of flames licked the roof. Now everyone could see the fire. No one was going to put it out.

Janie looked on in horror—she screamed at the grandstand. "Can't you see the tent is on fire!"

The sight and sound of the fire were not enough. Not until the third sensory perception, the furnace-like heat, boiled in their faces, did the crowd react. They all reacted at once. They struggled to stand. The bleachers rumbled under thousands of feet; folding chairs clattered and tangled together, a Coke bottle rolled down the aisle.

A mass hysteria gripped the crowd. All at once, eight thousand people surged forward to reach the exits. In the space of five seconds, Janie found herself in real danger of being trampled.

Outside, on the Barbour Street lot, hundreds of horrified neighbors and "townies" gathered and watched in collective horror as the roaring conflagration consumed the circus. As the big top burned, the tent acted like a chimney. One-hundred-foot tongues of flames shot up as the hot gases burst from the peak. The American flags continued to flap gallantly, fanned by the flames.

Behind a circle of red-painted wagons, Bobby Segee skulked. He waited for the stupid girl in the blue-checked dress to come out—he waited to finish what he'd started. After three minutes, a monstrously malevolent feeling of hate washed over him. "Burn, you little bitch, burn!"

"What'd yah say thar son?"

"I jest said, look at that son of a bitch burn."

The first tent pole toppled, trailing ropes and burning canvas. Janie frantically scanned the rows of general admission seats for a familiar face, her brother's face. What she saw instead was Holly J. and Wednesday sitting calmly in the audience with cones of fluffy pink cotton candy and matching green balloons.

"Holly J., Wednesday, where's Sid?" Janie shouted to make herself heard over the roar of the crowd.

"I dunno, your brother is a creep, we told him to scram!"

"I have to find Sid! Get out of here, can't you see the tent is on fire!" Janie screamed herself hoarse.

"Oh Janie, why must you always go and spoil everything? Come sit with us, the show will start back up any minute." Holly J. was forever bossy, and Wednesday didn't seem particularly worried either.

High overhead, chaotic 5 capered and pranced; it cachinnated with glee—frolicking on the wire abandoned by the Wallendas. The nihilist thing was in its glory.

Three minutes passed.

The crowd was in full panic now. Women screamed as their hair and dresses caught on fire. The heated paraffin from the roof not only burned, it melted and rained on the helpless circus fans, sticking to their flesh, burning like hot bacon fat.

One panicked man, thinking only about clearing a path for himself, wielded a folding chair like a machete. He hacked and chopped his way through the crowd, assailing women and children alike.

"Sidney!"

In an ocean of unfamiliar faces, at last, Janie spied her brother. Sid, 'the rat,' was seated halfway up on the middle tier. Her little brother was alone, lost and confused, tears streamed down his face. Paralyzed with fear, he still clutched his popcorn.

Impossibly, Janie found herself going the wrong way against the crowd. There were so many people all screaming and shoving, blocking her path; she didn't know how she was going to reach him. The plucky girl scaled the risers, skirting a tangled island of jumbled chairs, and tripped, scrambled, and clawed her way to the top of the grandstand.

The crazed man with the chair lashed out, knocking her to the ground. Twice more, Janie was bashed senseless and trampled—the determined girl regained her footing. The crowd surged forward and the narcissus man with the chair was swept away by the tide of panic. Janie never saw him again.

The fire reached the top of the center pole and split in three different directions. Panicked women and children ran in blind circles under the burning canvas and collided with each other in great numbers. In the chaotic crush, the terrified crowd bottlenecked against the steel-ribbed animal chutes, trampling hundreds. Holly J. and Wednesday sat passively and never moved from their seats. Their balloons burst from the heat.

Janie clutched her brother; Sidney cowered there in the chaos and clung to his sister, crying. She screamed in his face to be heard over the roar of the flames. "Sidney, we have to get out!"

"How?" The little boy trembled. He was beyond bewildered. Janie wasn't much better, but she pretended to be confident.

"I don't know, but I promise you, stay close to me." The surging mass of humanity blocked their way down. Escape anywhere but up was impossible. "We have to go higher!"

With strength she didn't know she possessed, Janie grabbed her brother by the hand and half-dragged, half-carried him across to the uppermost tier of the bleachers.

They were high enough now so they were level with the top of the sidewall, which hung partially slack to let in a breeze. Janie could see the promise of daylight through the gap. The way out was inches away; all that was left was to jump. The fifteen-foot drop from the top of the grandstand was daunting, but one look behind at the raging chaos and she knew it was the only way.

In a heroic effort to calm the crowd, Merle Evans and the band continued to play *"Stars and Stripes Forever,"* a scene eerily reminiscent of the string quintet playing to the end on the decks of the doomed Titanic.

"We have to jump!"

Sidney closed his eyes and shook his head. "It's too far!"

"You can do this—you have to jump—it's the only way!" Janie Firefly, jungle girl, intrepidly launched herself over the edge; always a bit of tomboy, she knew how to climb trees. She landed, knees bent, and rolled in the sawdust. She looked up, expecting Sid to follow.

"Jump, Sid!" Janie's panic heightened, her frightened brother refused to jump.

There wasn't time to argue. The heat was intense and the air temperature soared to over 500 degrees. The super-heated gasses burned their faces and made it impossible to breathe. If Janie couldn't persuade her brother to jump, and quick, they were both going to suffocate.

Before she had a chance to coax her brother down, the voracious fire flared. In one colossal gulp, the beast that was fire devoured a great gaping hole in the roof. The heavens opened up. Janie shielded her face; she could see open sky and the American flags flapping gallantly in the flaming cyclone. A flap of burning canvas fell from above. Great gouts of melted paraffin cascaded down; the thick globs of flaming wax landed, sizzling, on the girl's back and arms, burning her horribly.

Janie screamed. Sidney jumped.

Sidney tried to scrape away the molten terror but only managed to spread it around, burning his own hands in the process. A spotlight tore loose from the rigging and fell fifty feet, crashing into the grandstand; it bounced once and careened over the edge and landed with a thud next to the two children. The light missed Sidney completely, but a trailing piece of debris grazed the side of Janie's head.

"Sis!"

Janie crumpled to the ground. She tried to get back up, but her legs buckled. Her eyes rolled back in her head. Overcome with heat and smoke, she collapsed.

"Help me, 5!"

"Tsk, tsk." The id leaned, debonair, against a nineteenth-century gas-light stanchion, smoking a cigarette. Clad in an impeccable white dinner jacket and red carnation, an unknown companion sat waiting in the shadows. The immoral thing flashed a partially folded fifty-franc note. The garçon rushed to seat the creature at a most fashionable café table against the backdrop of the Seine River at the *Quai du Louvre* in Paris. 5 kissed the hand of its adulterous companion.

"Mais oui, mon cher mademoiselle, voulez-vous?" The number said in a surprisingly sophisticated continental accent and continued to behave as if it had all the time in the world.

"Help me, 5!" The villainous imp mocked its mistress —branded a nuisance and a pest one too many times—the anthropomorphic number ignored her pleas.

It could have helped, yet it chose to stand idle and do nothing, perfectly content to watch its mistress die.

Sidney wasn't going to let his sister die. The resourceful boy took out his jackknife, a birthday present from Uncle Bud, and slashed a gash in the canvas sidewall. He pulled on Janie with all his might, but the little boy wasn't strong enough to rouse his unconscious sister.

"Get up, Sis, please get up!"

Janie lay face-first in the sawdust. In a twilight, she felt herself being rolled over, lifted.

"She's hurt bad, help me get her up! We got to get out of here! Stay close to me, son." Sidney went first, followed by the unconscious girl in the arms of the clown.

Wicked 5 shrieked and spat, the perfidious imp screeched and gnashed its yellow teeth; it raved loathsome obscenities at the clown. "Bring her back! Let the little bitch burn!" The nihilist id chose not to follow—instead, it continued to dance and cavort in the flames, heedless to any danger posed by the gathering apocalyptic conflagration and its fiery crescendo.

Eight minutes passed.

Chapter 16

Two Tickets, Two Seconds

Death stalked the circus. The fire breached the roof of the big top—an enormous column of thick black smoke boiled up and cast a pernicious pall of death and destruction over the Barbour Street grounds. The chaos wrought in darkness, combined with the gasoline smell and the stench of burning human flesh, crafted a desolate triumvirate of misery, suffering, and death.

Sergeant Spellman sat in his police cruiser, sweltering in the stifling July heat. He opened the brown paper sack, what was left of his lunch, hoping his wife packed a second egg-salad sandwich. Plainclothesman John Brice leaned in the car window.

"Everything going okay, Frank?"

"A couple of pick-pockets, a lost child about an hour ago, pretty routine."

"Keep an eye out for those parole violators."

"Sure thing, Brice."

When Spellman opened his thermos, he heard the first screams from the tent. He thought a wild animal must have escaped. He took a bite of sandwich and reached under the seat to retrieve his shotgun.

Spellman continued to chew. The screams were louder now. He watched with increasing alarm as thousands of terrified spectators poured out of the exits. A fountainous geyser of flame shot up two hundred feet. The fire rent the roof like a blasphemous Roman candle. Spellman spat out his sandwich.

"Oh, shit!" A knot twisted in his stomach—his radio was broken, and he knew it. The patrolman abandoned his cruiser and sprinted across the midway to the first house on Barbour Street.

There was no telephone on the lot.

The first alarm signal came in at 2:44 PM. Engine Company no. 7, with two trucks, was the first to respond. One minute later, box 828 on Barbour Street tripped. Engine Companies 14, 4, and Truck 1 roared onto Kensington Street, lights and sirens blaring. The fire station was a scant mile-and-a-quarter from the circus grounds.

Pumper Engine no. 16 was the first to arrive. As they neared the intersection of Clark and Westland, two boys waved in the direction of the big top. From the moment they arrived, the firemen's efforts to combat the blaze were hampered. Elephants blocked the south entrance. Frantic bullmen shouted "Tails, tails," and the herd formed the familiar trunk-to-tail queue. The agitated elephants trumpeted. Agonizing seconds were lost as the handlers led the animals to safety.

Everywhere, obstacles blocked the firemen's path, screaming fans, stakes, crates, buckets, and barrels. The Coca-Cola tent caught fire. Hundreds of neatly arranged soda bottles exploded with a staccato chatter, spewing caramel fizz into the air. The intense heat from the fire melted the glass, and it pooled on the ground. The nearest fire hydrant was located across the street from McGovern's granite works. A thousand feet of fire hose snaked its way between the jumbled laager of circus wagons. It was already too late. The big top was fully engulfed.

Walter carried Janie some distance before he laid her gently on the grass in the relative calm of a shady grove of trees in Sponzo's orchard. The brave little girl's face was blackened with soot and her arms and back blistered where the flaming paraffin touched. Her beautiful blue and white-checkered dress singed to tatters, and gasoline vapor reeked noxious on her clothes.

"Lay quiet, kid, you're safe now." Walter feared the worst; the girl was hurt bad. The clown made a brief assessment of her injuries. Her skin was cold and clammy, a sure sign of shock. Walter elevated her legs and covered her with the jacket from his costume.

"Uncle Walt, where's Sid?" Janie said in a far-away voice. She drifted in and out of consciousness.

"Don't try to talk, sweetheart."

Janie struggled to sit up. The little girl had no comprehension of how seriously she was burned. "I have to go back. I have to find Sid!" Her battered head was spinning, she threw up.

"I'm here, Sis." Sidney squeezed his sister's hand. He tenderly wiped the vomit from her face—he didn't even say "ew" or nothing. "I love you, Sis, please don't die!" The sound of her brother's voice soothed Janie's worst fears. She closed her eyes. The adrenaline rush was gone, and the pain was starting to overtake her injured body. Walter checked her airway. She was still breathing.

There was a culmination of a crash and a roar. The circus tent did not so much collapse as it evaporated. Like mighty timber cut down in the forest, the heavy quarter-poles fell, one after another. The tallest center-pole was the last to fall. The guy ropes snapped; it wavered stoutheartedly before it, too, toppled and crashed to the ground, dragging with it the last remnants of blazing canvas, sisal, and rope. There rose up an eerie collective moan as the flaming canvas smothered the doomed souls still trapped under its embrace.

As quickly as it began, all was silent, save the pop and hiss of the flames.

One man, his wife, and their five-year-old daughter barely escaped the flames. Too young to understand what was happening, the little girl looked back and said, "It's a shame, it's a shame. The big tent."

The same scene played out all over the Barbour Street lot. People ran in panicked circles, screaming; some were still on fire. Grief-stricken parents searched for lost children; some prayed, others stood numb and watched as the blazing pyre slowly collapsed in a heap of cremated ruin.

A small boy wandered past, his clothing charred, his face blackened. He kept saying, "My mommy is going to come—my mommy is going to come . . ." His mother was never going to come home from the circus.

The entire tent, with all its poles, was gone. No part of the circus top was spared, every section, every steel rail, every steel cage was blackened, bent, and charred to calx. Even the bandstand, at the farthest point from where the fire began, a full five hundred feet, was calcined to a charred, twisted wreck.

"Don't look, honey." Walter covered Janie's eyes. "I've been in show business twenty years, kid." The clown's voice choked, "I've been through storms, floods, blowdowns, and train wrecks. My god, I ain't never seen nothing like this!"

Somehow, amid the madness, Charlie found Walter and Sidney huddled with Janie at the edge of Sponzo's meadow. Thanks to the two tickets and the front-row seats, Charlie's own escape from death had been relatively easy, but the boy was so badly traumatized, even in later years, he never sat in an audience again.

"Is she hurt bad, mister?"

"I'm afraid so, son," Walter said. He was genuinely relieved that the older boy was there. Now it was safe to leave the children. "You wait here with Sidney. Try to keep her quiet. I'm going to go find some help."

"Janie, it's Charlie . . ." Janie never opened her eyes.

* * *

Janie sat up.

"Janie, you crazy upidstay girl, you're alive!" Charlie hugged her with all his might. Then Charlie did something he never thought he'd do in ten million years, and he certainly never would have done had he thought about it. He kissed her. The strangest thing about it was after he kissed her, he wasn't sorry, and kissed her again for good measure. His friend was alive!

Charlie's exultant joy was suddenly tempered with an awful, sobering reality. Before he found them, he'd overheard a police officer questioning the chief usher.

"*. . . Yeah, a little girl, blonde hair, about so high, blue-checked dress, not more than eleven or twelve, I reckon. She said something about a fire in the men's washroom.*"

"Janie, the police are looking for you. I seen a policeman questioning the ushers. They think you set the fire!" Charlie said in a voice so hushed it was barely audible. The thought, the mere possibility, that his best friend burned down the big top was too awful to contemplate. "Tell me the truth. Did 5 start the fire?"

"Chucky, how can you say such awful things? 5 didn't have nothing to do with it. I swear!"

Charlie wasn't so sure.

"It was Bobby Segee set the fire. I seen him do it!" Charlie didn't believe her— she could see it in his eyes. Janie trembled with grief. She was a liar, and she knew it. The awful reality of the accusation conflicted profoundly with the truth. *She was telling the truth!* Janie didn't know how to convince Charlie this wasn't just another one of her horrible lies. She'd done some naughty things in her life, but never, ever, did she do anything so wicked and awful as this. Janie began to weep inconsolably.

"Crissy Greene, she's dead. He killed her! I think he thought Crissy was me, 'cos when he figured she wasn't—that's when he lit after me. He said he was gonna kill me!"

There was a tinge of credibility in Janie's revelation; at last, he believed her. Charlie felt stupid, stupid for having accused his friend. "We have to go to the police."

"Oh no, we can't do that! Chucky, I'm so scared."

"All those people dead—we can't let him get away with this! We have to tell somebody."

Janie shook her head.

"Okay, we'll talk to Mr. Paradise. Mr. Paradise, he'll know what to do."

Janie wasn't listening. "I've got to get away—I've got to run away!"

Charlie wasn't about to let his friend go anywhere. He wrestled with the upidstay girl. "Stop it! Janie, listen to me, the tent is gone."

"No, you don't understand. Holly J. and Wednesday are still in there. I've got to go back!"

Janie struggled to get away.

"Janie, please! I'm your friend and I love you!" The words popped out of Charlie's mouth. The surprised boy couldn't believe what he'd just said. The commitment was so profound, it called into question every neurotic inhibition, every neurosis he'd ever suffered in his whole life. Not until he said the words out loud did he realize the depth of feelings he held for the girl.

"Janie, I love you. Not the same way you love me—maybe love isn't even the right word." Charlie resisted his emotions. "Let's just say, I really, really like you—if you love me—You'll do this for me. Forget about Holly J. and Wednesday." Charlie squeezed Janie's hand tight in his fist.

"Do you feel that?"

"You're hurting me."

"That's 'cos I'm real. Those other people, they don't exist. They're all in your head."

"They're real to me," Janie said in a deliberate voice. "I love you, Chucky." Tears filled Janie's eyes. "Chucky, I'm sorry . . ." and she kicked Charlie in the shin, and was at once very sorry. She kicked him so hard, Charlie felt his tibia crack. The surprised boy was hobbled.

"Janie, come back! Don't do this, please come back!" Janie never looked back. The crazy girl took off running in the direction of the flaming tent. Charlie was the last person to see her alive.

"Uncle Walt says the ambulance is on its way . . ." Sidney discovered Charlie sitting alone on the ground, rubbing his shin. "Sis is gone, isn't she?" The little boy recognized the awful truth etched on Charlie's face. The two boys sat in the grass, held each other, and cried.

* * *

All afternoon they searched. It was two hours before the smoldering rubble was cool enough to search. Janie didn't come home. Janie Firefly was never coming home.

Forty-eight hours after she disappeared, Janie was officially declared missing. Her body was never recovered. No one held out any realistic hope that the girl was still alive.

The time came to face the unthinkable.

There were so many dead that the State Armory was the only building in Hartford large enough to serve as a makeshift morgue. Jim Paradise scanned the list of names of dead and missing. His finger trembled as he traced down the "M" column with a terrible sense of dread.

Marcovicz, Francis Jr. Marcovicz, Stephanie
Marcus, Martin
Mason, Jarvis W.
Mason, Marcia McKinney
Mather, Lola Booth
Mather, Sarah Elizabeth
Matteson, Theresa E.
Matthews, Dorothy C.
Matthews, Roslyn
McConaughey, Jane E.
Mearman, Charlotte
Metcalf, Marjorie R.
Miles, Monica
Milliken, Stephen Ronald
Moor, Martha Ann
Murphy, Charles Walter
Murphy, Hortense
Murphy, Walter D.

Chapter 17

Little Girl Lost

The attendant pulled back the sheet. The little girl lay on the cot, naked; she was a beautiful child, serene even in death, her face barely touched by the fire. The girl had delicate features and light brown hair, which reached down to her shoulders. All that was known about her was spelled out on her morgue tag in terse forensic jargon:

<u>1565</u>
Unidentified white female, age: approximately six years,
height: 3'10" weight: 40 lbs., eyes: blue,
build: moderately well-developed,
hair: shoulder-length, blonde or light-brown, curly.

She was a young girl, not more than six years old, younger than Janie, for that Jim was thankful. A thirty-year arson investigator, he'd seen his share of dead bodies, but the body of a dead child never ceased to shock. Jim shook his head. This was not the girl. He dared a final glance at the child. Only slightly burned on one cheek, surely she would be identified and taken home soon.

Robert McConaughey was in Washington in a meeting with the Army Chief-of-Staff and Mrs. McConaughey, when she heard the news, was so overcome with grief she had to be sedated. Jim volunteered to help the family and perform the grim duty of identifying Janie.

Escorted by a Red Cross volunteer, Jim Paradise made his way across the cavernous drill floor of the State Armory. He went immediately to the section designated "Children—Female." It was here that Jim first noticed her. He was drawn at once to her innocent face. "Such a beautiful child," Jim said.

The sight of the little girl lost, lying so peacefully, was disconsolate. The tiny child seemed almost to be sleeping, a perception of which made the stark reality of the unknown child's death all the more difficult to accept.

Jim shook his head. This girl was not Janie.

Jim continued his bleak quest, thirty cots, thirty tiny shrouded bodies. Jim's resolve was tested to the breaking point. It was almost more than he could bear. Each time the sheet was pulled back, he felt a "Russian roulette" sense of relief. No, this child was not Janie. He was shown the final unknown child. The silent shape lay on the cot filled his heart with a solemn dread. His legs trembled, he could hardly bring himself to look.

"We didn't undress her," the morgue attendant's voice was flat and impersonal. "She's pretty badly burned . . . 1503, unknown juvenile female, white, approximately twelve-years-old, four foot two inches, seventy-five pounds, cause of death, fourth-degree burns, no sign of traumatic internal injuries."

The corpse that confronted him, 1503, was scarcely human. Jim could see right away the tiny body was about Janie's height and weight. On her left foot was a saddle shoe, and on her breast, a charred tatter of a blue-and-white checked dress, a pitiful reminder of her past life, now lost. Jim knew at once, he collapsed to his knees.

"Oh, mein poor fräulein, Janie . . . Janie Firefly, I'm so sorry." The old man wept inconsolably. Jim was so overcome with grief, he had to be escorted from the armory.

* * *

In a semicircle of brightly-painted red Ringling wagons, untouched by the fire, Bobby Segee shared no such grief. He admired his handiwork. The fire was so catastrophic, so complete was the destruction wrought, that on a primitive level, it frightened even him. He saw the tall clown with the white face, his make-up smudged and streaked with tears, searching, calling her name. Segee savored the moment. They were looking for her. The stupid little cunt was as good as dead.

Bobby rifled a woman's purse, dropped by one of his hundreds of nameless, faceless victims. He turned it inside out, dumping the content on the ground. There was five dollars.

Six Ringling officials were arrested. Bobby took special pleasure as he watched his boss, Whitey Versteeg, led away in handcuffs. In the first twenty-four hours, the incompetent investigation remained blindsided, completely focused on management negligence and the "dropped cigarette theory." Law enforcement officials never detained him, no detective ever questioned him. No suspicions were ever cast on Segee or his shadowy past. No one considered the possibility that a deadly arsonist had infiltrated the Ringling troupe. Neither was any link established to the two previous suspicious fires by Commissioner Hickey or the Connecticut State arson investigators. Bobby Segee slipped through the cracks.

Segee laughed a cruel, wicked laugh. All afternoon, he watched them carry out the blackened corpses; he paid special attention to the child-size corpses. He couldn't believe his dumb luck. He cackled again; he had nothing to fear. There was only one witness to his monstrous crime, the McConaughey girl, and she was missing. Only she knew the truth, and the little bitch was dead.

By nine o'clock, it became too dark to continue the search. They cordoned off the Barbour Street lot. No one paid any attention to him. It was a simple matter for one evil, sixteen-year-old boy with a terrible black secret to slip quietly out of town. Five dollars put him on a bus bound for Portland, Maine. Bobby Segee never returned to Hartford.

* * *

Merle Evans and his band continued to play for the survivors just outside the tent. Parents wandered past, weeping, searching for lost children.

"I saw it! Some son-of-a-bitch flicked a cigarette!" Graflex Speed Graphics popped and flashed; the man reveled in his instant celebrity. Reporters from as far away as Sacramento mobbed him, hung on his every word. With that single utterance, the "dropped cigarette" theory gained credible traction. Rumor and hearsay became fact and crystallized into a collective hysteria. The theory became preeminent in the minds of Commissioner Hickey, Chief-of-Police Hallissey, and State attorney H. M. Alcorn.

"Not possible." Jim Paradise flatly contradicted. "I checked with the national weather bureau. The humidity yesterday at two o'clock, the time of the fire, was forty-three percent." Jim knew from experience, and contrary to popular belief, cigarettes are a notoriously poor source of ignition, especially in conditions of high humidity.

"The seatmen are wrong." The circus employees positioned under the grandstand for the nominal purpose of retrieving lost umbrellas, or in this case, an errant cigarette, were not, in his determination, the best witnesses to the cause of the fire. Jim tapped his notebook. Maybe the authorities weren't interested, but he was. He knew how to investigate a fire. He tracked down and interviewed them all, and was prepared to back up his claim with twenty pages of detailed notes.

Jim's frustration turned to anger as it became increasingly clear, Hickey wasn't qualified to investigate candles on a birthday cake—let alone a fire of this scope and magnitude. Commissioner Hickey was a politician with no prior arson investigation experience. Hickey was more concerned with political fallout than he was about facts. The dropped cigarette theory was neat and tidy and, for the time being, explained everything.

Without official sanction, Jim's efforts were stymied. His citizen investigation was unwelcome as it was unheeded. "None of the seatmen reported any smoldering; no one smelled smoke. It's now 2:40, the curtain sidewall and leading edge of the roof are already involved."

Hickey scoffed.

"Commissioner, grass fires cannot start in conditions above seventeen percent humidity. This was no grass fire, no dropped cigarette. This was arson."

"Who the hell are you? I am in authority here. Get out of here!" Hickey's face soured. The commissioner's patience was starting to wear thin. He was fed up with this outsider, this heinie, kraut, Jim Paradise, and his big-shot New York investigations.

Sheriff Ficano personally escorted Jim off the property.

Jim Paradise wasn't finished. Bulldog Jim's next stop was the office of Chief Medical Examiner, Dr. Weissenborn.

"What do you mean, no autopsy?"

"I assure you, Mr. Paradise, no autopsy is necessary. All the victims died of the same thing: burns, trampling, and smoke inhalation. The temperature inside the tent reached 1500 degrees. It's all the same. Please, Mr. Paradise, can't we just get on with it."

"No, we can't. I need you to do your job, Doctor."

"How, please, tell me?" Dr. Weissenborn scoffed, "This is Hartford, maybe you do things a little differently in New York. State law is quite clear. I am within my authority. I've already signed the death certificates. I'm telling you, as Chief Medical Examiner of Hartford County, all the victims died of burns and traumatic blunt force. Trampling, if you prefer."

"Except this one," Jim couldn't bring himself to say "unknown" or worse yet, the number 1503.

"Doctor, three more deceased arrived from Municipal," the morgue technician interrupted.

"One-hundred and twenty-two dead," Weissenborn said. His countenance was grim. "As you can see, we're overwhelmed, understaffed. I'm a busy man. Will there be anything else?"

"One more thing, Doctor, the body found by the men's toilets. Commissioner Hickey correctly identified that as the area of the fire's origin. It's possible the victim was still alive and witnessed the arsonist set the blaze."

"I'm tired of you and your Sam Spade conspiracies. Get out of here, you're wasting my time."

"I know who she is . . ."

"That's impossible!" For the first time, Dr. Weissenborn showed a hint of human emotion. He quickly regained his composure and resumed his non-committal, clinical stonewall. "1503 is burned beyond all recognition. The decedent died of fourth-degree burns. Please, I don't have time for this. Do we have to go over this again? It's all settled; the unknowns are scheduled to be buried tomorrow."

"It might make a great deal of difference," Jim said. He put on a pair of white gloves, and from a manila envelope, he removed a fragment of a blue-checked dress. "I bought the dress."

"Where did you get that?"

"Where I got the fragment is not the issue. The fräulein's name is Jane Elizabeth McConaughey. According to the coroner's field report, the majority of the dead were found crushed next to the steel animal chutes, this body is the exception. It was found alone, less than twenty feet from an exit. The victim was not trampled, you said so yourself. There are no signs of blunt traumatic injury."

Dr. Weissenborn appeared nervous.

"I know this fräulein. Janie is a smart girl. Unless she was incapacitated somehow, she would have escaped. Something or someone prevented her from escaping. I believe the fräulein was murdered."

The word *murder* caused Dr. Weissenborn's face to go pale. "More speculations on your part. This is not a murder investigation. There isn't going to be any murder investigation. Good afternoon, Mr. Paradise." Weissenborn picked up a clipboard and began taking notes. Jim could see the writing on the tablet, nothing but scribbles. The little weasel was making fake notes.

"We're not finished here, Dr. Weissenborn. The fräulein wasn't crushed or trampled . . ."

"Are you a doctor?" Weissenborn became testy.

"I'm a retired police detective. I've seen my share of crime scenes. The fräulein wasn't stabbed or shot, these are facts. Someone killed this mädchen. There's a high probability she was strangled."

"What do you want, Mr. Paradise? I don't know what you want."

"I want justice for mein Janie. I want justice for the one hundred other people who were murdered. I'm asking you to do the autopsy." Jim grabbed the doctor by the wrist. He was stronger than the doctor. Jim's eyes were full of light. "We need to be sure." Jim faced down the doctor. The Luger pistol tucked in his waistband weighed heavy on his conscience.

"Get out of here before I call the police!"

"Maybe we should both call the police. You're going to do this autopsy."

"I refuse. An autopsy will prove nothing!"

"What are you afraid of, Doctor? Afraid you'll find no soot in her lungs? You know as well as I do, if there's no inhaled soot in the victim's lungs, then the fräulein was dead before the fire began. Therefore, she must have died another way. Only an autopsy will tell us if the victim's hyoid bone is broken. Then we'll know for certain if Janie died in the fire—or was murdered."

"Stop it, quit calling her that!" Dr. Weissenborn was visibly disconcerted. His hand shook. "You don't know who she is. Nobody does! Can't you get it through your thick kraut head? This girl was not murdered!"

"You motherless schweinehund! Janie didn't die in the fire. Janie died before the fire . . . And you, Herr Doktor, don't have just another unknown fire victim. You have the largest mass murder in US history."

Chapter 18

Hartford 1944

Holly J. was dead. Wednesday too, perished, screaming. Janie shielded her face from the heat. The boiling smell of gasoline and the screams of the dying assaulted her senses. The big top was in its final seconds.

"Little girl, get back!"

Janie did not get back. She did not turn away. There was a great roar, the ground shook as the center-pole toppled, dragging with it the last remnants of flaming tarpaulin. Sparks burned her cheeks. There, amid the hecatomb of burning canvas, paraffin, and ruin, she caught sight of something moving in hell's center ring, a last glimpse of wicked 5, shrieking and dancing with death.

5 did not depart willingly. Treacherous to the last, the baneful number screeched havoc and from hell's own heart, a pernicious claw clutched and stabbed her soul. Janie kicked and fought back. The malicious id succumbed at last, and plunged, baying, into the abyss. Janie turned her back. There was a closing of a door, a great burden was cast aside, and the girl bobbed to the surface of the black water and took her first, free breath. 5 was gone. Extinguished forever—consumed in the purifying pyre of its own wickedness.

Janie felt a great silence in her head. Thousands of terrified people continued to mob the Barbour Street lot, yet she felt terribly alone. Numb with grief, suffocated by a spectacle of death and suffering so great in magnitude it was beyond her ability to comprehend. All afternoon she watched them carry out the black bodies until she couldn't stand to watch another minute. So great was her sorrow, she thought her heart would burst. Hundreds of innocent people dead, and for no reason other than Bobby Segee's invidious requital to murder.

It was all her fault. Janie did what she always did when she didn't know what else to do. She ran away. She was still running away. The deafening silence in her head was poised to drive her mad. For the first time in her life, her mind was clear. She was free of the psychosis that had tormented her for eleven years. Janie felt free, and yet at the same time she felt cold, desolate, and utterly alone. She stopped running.

* * *

Janie looked down. She could see herself floating in a white room. Everything around her was shimmering white. She wanted to stay because she felt so full of joy and peace. She could see a bright light. She tried to go towards the light, when she tried to move her right arm, her whole body felt like it was made of lead. She saw a man's face in the light. She thought it might be Saint Peter come to welcome her home. She'd always imagined Peter as a much older man, she remembered seeing his picture in *The Book of Knowledge*. Wasn't Peter supposed to have a beard?

I sure hope they take Methodists.

"Oh, crud!" No naked cherubs, cherubim and seraphim, pearly gates, or celestial angels playing harps of gold. Nope, none of that, nothing but a crummy hospital bed in room 501 of Hartford Municipal hospital. It was all a colossal disappointment.

"She's coming around," Dr. Haralson said.

"Wake up, honey." Janie opened her eyes and looked into the loving face of her mother. The room was white, the nurses and doctors all wore white.

"Is this heaven?"

"She's still dopey from the morphine," the doctor said. Sidney laughed when the doctor said his sister was dopey.

"Be quiet, Sidney."

The doctor shined a light in her eyes; he wore one of those ocular silver reflectors. He checked her reflexes. "She's been in a coma for four days. With these kinds of head injuries, we expect to see some disorientation and confusion."

"I love you, Sis." Sidney laid his head on his sister's breast and sobbed silently. Janie was bandaged like a mummy. She reached out to her brother with her one good hand and smoothed his hair.

"You look like King Tut, Sis!"

"You know what?—I love you, too—even if you are a rat!"

"Aw, shove it!"

"You better watch out or I'll come back and haunt you."

Janie's faint, mischievous grin displayed none of her usual sparkle. She sunk back down on her pillow. She felt weak but deeply satisfied. Her relationship with her brother had returned to normal, no more mushy stuff. Come to think about it, she liked it better that way.

* * *

"Doctor," Janie said in a small voice, "Will I ever be able to play the piano?"

"You're a brave little girl. With your courage and determination, I don't see any reason why not."

"Gee that's great doc, I never could play before!"

Charlie laughed. Janie had lost none of her sense of humor. The upidstay girl was still stealing his jokes, but this time, he didn't even mind.

"I'm afraid your daughter faces months of therapy and rehabilitation." Doctor Haralson turned to her father. "Pneumonia and secondary infection is always our biggest concern, we've been giving her penicillin, but there's not enough to go around. There was no damage to her hand, but she'll need skin grafts on her back and arm."

Her whole family rallied around her. Janie still had no idea she'd been burned in the fire.

"Janie, I'm here." Charlie squeezed his friend's hand.

"Chucky, I'm sorry I kicked you."

Charlie looked on curiously, "Don't be so upidstay, you never kicked me."

"Oh, that's good." Janie felt a sense of relief, "'cos if'n I did kick you, I didn't mean it, honest."

Janie paused. It all seemed so real. She couldn't remember very much about what happened. She remembered being in her father's study. She remembered calling the fire department. Everything else was a murky blank. The one thing she was positive about was kicking her best friend. She distinctly remembered because of how much she deeply regretted it afterward. Now Janie was more confused than ever. If that didn't happen, maybe none of it happened.

She shuddered at the sight of Bobby Segee's hateful face. She thought she remembered something about the boy, something terrible, something evil. Her mind was a muffled cloud. How could she ever be sure? The one thing she knew for certain: 5 was gone, extirpated. Wednesday and Holly J. too, were dead, for that Janie felt very sad. She was determined to put Bobby Segee and wicked 5 out of her mind forever.

"You gave us quite a scare."

"I love you, Daddy. When can I go home? I wanna go home." She tried to sit up. A wave of pain encircled her and held her in its vise. She clutched the railing on her bed. "It hurts."

"Doctor! Lay quiet, sweetheart, the doctor will give you something for the pain. There was a fire, darling . . . you were at the circus, don't you remember anything?"

There was no recollection in Janie's eyes. Robert looked to the doctor, alarmed. "She doesn't remember?"

"I suspect there's some post-traumatic amnesia," Dr. Haralson said. "These things sometimes clear up with time and in her case, maybe it's better if she never remembers."

"Janie, there's someone here to see you."

"Uncle Walt!"

"Hi'ya, kid." Walter kissed her forehead. "How's my little lightning bug? Everybody's asking about you." With a flair of legerdemain, the clown produced a bouquet of paper flowers from his sleeve.

Janie smiled. She reached up and touched the clown's face. "I love you, Uncle Walt. I'm sorry. I'm sorry I ran away and worried everybody."

"Don't cry, sweetheart—you cry, then I cry."

"Uncle Walt?" Janie said, her voice still weepy. "If I promise to be good and never, ever, run away ever again, can I come to Sarasota on the first of May? I want to go on the road with you and Em . . . I never did get to be a lion tamer."

"A lion tamer, huh?" Walter chuckled. "You still got that idea stuck in your pretty little head?" Walter was disconcerted. "The kid doesn't remember a thing, huh?" No one made eye contact. The feeling in the room was incommodious. Robert stared at the floor and shook his head.

"Aw shucks, at least some things haven't changed, the kid still wants to be a lion tamer."

"It's the morphine," Dr. Haralson said.

"Sure kid, we're an act. One thing I know for sure, you'll be the gosh darn prettiest lion tamer the Big Show ever had!" Walter pretended to be upbeat. His face betrayed none of his true sorrow but his heart was breaking. She had no idea her beloved circus lay in ashes. The little girl almost died because of him and two tickets.

Ninety-eight people dead the first day, twenty-two more these last four days, and the butcher's bill was still not satisfied. Walter was glad she couldn't remember. He wished he could forget. He wasn't about to crush the sweet child's dreams, there was plenty of time for her to learn the terrible facts. There was nothing left of the big show. The circus was in ruins, six men in jail, and the Ringling circus in receivership. He was out of a job. He wasn't even sure if there was going to be a "next year."

"We'll work something out. You get better now, you hear. We'll worry about next year, next year."

The little girl looked weary and very far away. "I think I'd like to sleep now." Janie closed her eyes and sailed off on a river of crystal light with Wynken, Blynken, and Nod in a morphine-induced embrace.

* * *

The house on 625 Elm Street was exactly as she remembered it. The prelude to New England's fall colors was in the air and the day was especially full of promise. This was her first time out of the house. She looked very pretty in her new fall dress Grams had brought from Chicago. She walked up the driveway very slowly, each step measured by pain. Jim Paradise sat on his front porch smoking his pipe. A copy of the *Hartford Courant* lay on the table beside him.

U.S. TROOPS CROSS SIEGFRIED LINE,
ENTER GERMANY.

There was no word from his sons, Ernst and Fritz. His heart was heavy. "Helloo, Mr. Paradise!" "Mein gott! Mein poor dear fräulein!" Jim sunk to his knees and hugged Janie tenderly in his strong arms. "Janie, you look so well, please telling me you have not been a naughty little girl, running away, no?"

"Oh no sir, my daddy dropped me off. The doctor said I can't start school in the fall. I'm 'invalid.' I have to have another operation."

"Mein poor brave Janie."

"Chucky's going to bring my homework every day, now I'll never be late for school!"

"That's fine, Herr Charlie is a good boy."

"Is ze jung mädchen staying for ze supper? I making ze strudel." Frau Detweiler smiled from behind the sanctuary of the screen door. She kept smiling.

Janie hobbled onto the porch, her arm in a sling. Her hair was longer and combed to one side to hide the burns on her face. Her body was scarred, but her spirit remained bright and her dimpled smile sparkled as ever.

"I've got new shoes." Janie showed off her black Mary Jane shoes. "My other shoes got burnt up."

Jim admired her shoes and her pretty, navy blue argyle sweater and matching blue skirt. "Grams bought 'em at Marshall Fields in Chicago. Have you ever been to Chicago, Mr. Paradise?"

"Ja, I going to the Chicago. Frau, now that our Janie is here, please fetching the *geschank*."

"What have you got? Something for me, Mr. Paradise?" Janie was excited.

"A present for your well-getting, fräulein." Jim smiled, his eyes twinkled. The cardboard box was mysterious and poked full of holes. The box quivered and shook with anticipation.

Janie could scarcely contain her curiosity. She tore open the brown paper and lifted the lid. Curled up inside was a kitten, a real live cat!

"Oh, Mr. Paradise, you're the most wonderful friend in the whole world!" She hugged the old man. "I love you." Janie cuddled the kitten. It was already purring. Her very own gray and black tabby cat, no more made-up imaginary cats!

"Telling me Janie Firefly, what will you call your new friend?"

Janie didn't hesitate. "It's Janie . . . just plain Janie, and his name is Seven."

END

EPILOGUE

HARTFORD 1944 is fiction. The historical individuals and locations portrayed herein are fiction. What is true is that 168 innocent people died on that tragic day of July 6, 1944. Writing this novel has proven to be an emotional journey. As I gathered my notes, as I did more research, these people became increasingly real to me. I was drawn to their story with a profound sense of reverence. I felt a duty to proceed carefully to avoid trivializing their tragic loss by the juxtaposition of my fictional story against the backdrop of their deaths.

This is a story that needs to be told. A uniquely American tragedy equal in scope to the Titanic or Hindenburg—yet it remains largely a forgotten chapter in American history. Perhaps, like so many others, what I wanted was answers. In writing this novel, it is my endeavor to bring a measure of closure in a fictional context where the courts, arson investigators, and law enforcement officials failed.

Bobby Segee is a real person. There exists substantial credible evidence that Segee murdered three children before the time he turned sixteen. There is circumstantial evidence that Segee acted willfully, maliciously, in starting the Hartford circus fire, including the arsonist's own confession and his past propensity for setting fires. If this is true, this makes Robert Dale Segee the greatest un-indicted mass murderer in US history. Segee was ultimately arrested in Ohio in 1951 for setting a grain elevator on fire.

S. Michael McAllister

www.ingramcontent.com/pod-product-compliance
Lightning Source LLC
Chambersburg PA
CBHW021434150726
47989CB00001B/249